Confronting Counterinsurgency

Cop Cities and Democracy's Terrors

Edited by Joy James

PLUTO PRESS

First published 2025 by Pluto Press
New Wing, Somerset House, Strand, London WC2R 1LA
and Pluto Press, Inc.
1930 Village Center Circle, 3-834, Las Vegas, NV 89134

www.plutobooks.com

British Library Cataloguing in Publication Data
A catalogue record for this book is available from the British Library

ISBN 978 0 7453 5154 4   Paperback
ISBN 978 0 7453 5156 8   PDF
ISBN 978 0 7453 5155 1   EPUB

This book is printed on paper suitable for recycling and made from
fully managed and sustained forest sources. Logging, pulping and
manufacturing processes are expected to conform to the environmental
standards of the country of origin.

Typeset by Stanford DTP Services, Northampton, England

Simultaneously printed in the United Kingdom and United States of
America

EU GPSR Authorized Representative
LOGOS EUROPE, 9 rue Nicolas Poussin, 17000, LA ROCHELLE,
France
Email: Contact@logoseurope.eu

Confronting Counterinsurgency

"This is an essential and incendiary political and philosophical reflection on current global resistance movements. A collection of powerful narratives rooted in the liberation strategies of those who struggle against corporate and state conquest, brutality and death and who continue to resist."

—Ken Fero, radical filmmaker and convenor of
The People's Tribunal on Police Killings

"Makes plain the relations between the U.S. as a militarized carceral police state, the imprisonment of our resistance, and the genocidal wars our technocracy imparts to the world in Gaza and beyond. This is a work of radical care and love, a study guide for the urgency of the moment where we must fight, to live, and to struggle."

—Dian Million, author of *Therapeutic Nations:*
Healing in an Age of Indigenous Human Rights

"True to its title, this eye-opening book holds its readers steady while guiding us through a perturbing confrontation with counterinsurgency in empire's proxy wars, colonies, prisons and schools. Cop cities emerge as domestic forts to contain an unlikely enemy — us. But we're neither helpless, nor alone."

—Frances Madeson, writer, author of *Cooperative Village*

"A powerful collection that reminds us that the progress we build toward liberation must be constantly defended. Rooted in a radical sense of love, care, and self-critique, this collection brings together necessary conversations and analyses surrounding our movements."

—Momodou Taal, *The Malcolm Effect* Podcast

"*Confronting Counterinsurgency* is woven to form a radical tapestry that leads the reader into and through vibrant sites of insurgency, life-making, and struggle against the crushing force of fascism, imperial rot, and racial capitalism."

—Lara Sheehi, author of *From the Clinic to the Streets:*
Psychoanalysis for Revolutionary Futures

"Spanning geographies and different approaches to organizing, these essays consistently demonstrate that the struggle for abolition is a global Black struggle. Abolition breaches the gates of reformist logics of all sorts to articulate a radical account of community-making and to offer us a different account of what living better collectively together can be."

—Rinaldo Walcott, author of *On Property:*
Policing, Prisons, and the Call for Abolition

Joy James, Ebenezer Fitch Professor of the Humanities at Williams College, is a political philosopher who works with organizers. She is editor of *The Angela Y. Davis Reader*, *Imprisoned Intellectuals*, and co-editor of *The Black Feminist Reader*. James's recent books include: *In Pursuit of Revolutionary Love*, *New Bones Abolition*, and *Contextualizing Angela Davis*. Her edited volumes with Pluto also include *Beyond Cop Cities* and *ENGAGE: Indigenous, Black, Afro-Indigenous Futures*.

[F]ascism cannot exist without a national security state and without an authoritarian form of government that has a national police force at its disposal. From the day we were brought here, the African community in the United States has been living under a version of fascism. We have this Frankenstein version of fascism here in America, because we have the merger of democracy—so-called democratic institutions—with the corporate, militarized state. Fascism has always been the marriage or the unity between finance capital, the rich, corporations and the state. It's the state that has the monopoly on violence. It's the state that can legally kill people literally. It's the state that can control dissent. Without a national police force, fascism is almost impossible.

—Dhoruba Bin-Wahad, *Revolution in These Times*

Contents

Abbreviations

AEH	Agreement to End Hostilities
AIM	American Indian Movement
BAR	*Black Agenda Report*
BIPOC	Black, Indigenous and People of Color
BLA	Black Liberation Army
BLM	Black Lives Matter
BPM	Black Power Media
CDCR	California Department of Corrections and Rehabilitation
CIA	Central Intelligence Agency
CPUSA	Communist Party USA
CRC	Civil Rights Congress
DOD	Department of Defense
DRC	Democratic Republic of the Congo
FBI	Federal Bureau of Investigation
GBI	Georgia Bureau of Investigation
GILEE	Georgia International Law Enforcement Exchange
ICE	Immigration and Customs Enforcement
ISIS	Islamic State in Iraq and Syria
MOUT	Military Operations on Urban Terrain
NBA	National Basketball Association
NYPD	New York Police Department
PHRM	Prisoner Human Rights Movement
POTUS	President of the United States
RCGP	Restricted Custody General Population
RICO	Racketeer Influenced and Corrupt Organizations Act
SHU	Security Housing Units
SOA	School of the Americas
SRO	School Resource Officer
SVD	Silicon Valley De-Bug
SWAT	Special Weapons and Tactics
UN	United Nations

Preface

Chores Can Mitigate Casualties

Before cell phones, refrigerator magnets alerted us to our scheduled obligations. Those "privileged" to be housed and fed, sought nourishment in the kitchen and were greeted by fridge signage reminders of bills due, medical appointments, grocery runs, house/work repairs, picking up or dropping off children, supporting the elderly and the fragile. We have also posted notes-to-self that warn of wars in real time and space, or seen on screens. We emerge deeply traumatized, mourning the martyred and the casualties of wars. Those who go forward to resist predatory warfare will integrate daily responsibilities into war resistance and myriad attempts to slow crawl a fascist state, one that cultivates cruelty to be embedded in US democracy. Increasingly, our magnets align with weekly alphabets of resistance. Each day in the kitchen, greeting functions that deter repression, persecution and discrimination, we see or imagine monsters mixing meth (Hitler's Third Reich mass murderers were high, as was the Fuhrer)[1] in order to endure their killing sprees. Monday–Sunday fridge letters can help us to refocus on—and not freak out about—the state-corporation's ultra-violent shedding of life.

The meanings of our days and nights are calculated in the percentages of resistance written in shorthand rebel chores. Born in an apocalypse of enslavement and war, Captive Maternals constantly clean up others' messes, including leaky and moldy fridges. Stepping into caretaking, protesting, movements, marronage, war resistance, and sanctuary building, we stabilize and structure each day: M = Monday = *Monsters*; T = Tuesday = *Terrors*; W = Wednesday = *Wars*; Th = Thursday = *Tribunals*; F = Friday = *Freedoms*; S = Saturday = *Struggles*; S = Sunday = *Sanctuaries*. Laborers- and warriors-as-resisters dedicate their calendar days to education, politics, spirituality—all forms of liberation tutorials.[2]

Protesting in front of the fridge, or in front of police barricades, we dare to bridge the epicenter's surface politics in order to move towards the hypocenter's ground zero of revolutionary struggle. POTUSES who radiate hedonistic horrors will always poison the fridge. Their Caligula[3] vibes kill our rights, natural environments, freedoms—thus shortening various aspects of our lives. U.S. presidents weave an expansive "counterinsurgency" that stalks and undermines revolutionary struggles, decolonization, labor rights and clean environs, as well as protections to the nonbinary/trans/queer, wo/man, child, elderly, neurodiverse, impoverished and racially stigmatized.

The daily attempts to evade a moldy fridge, an airtight coffin for ideological slime and slow suffocation through liberalism, neoliberalism, conservatism, and neoconservatism—enable the isms that have slid into (proto)fascisms. Barbarity is indigestible. Choking or vomiting on reactionary political leftovers, the compassionate and committed demand healthy fare, clean air/water/soil. This food fight is a battle for life that states and corporations have jeopardized, shortened or stolen.

Steered into an infectious petri dish, democracy sinks into a moldy fridge. We are obligated to scrub or dismantle the poisonous incubators and the authoritarian motor that drives it. Hence, our communities will continue to scrutinize and double-check our calendars in order to schedule engagements that labor for, and leverage, revolutionaries who love more than we fear.

— Joy James, April 27, 2025

Introduction

Joy James

This collection builds upon and travels beyond the 2024 volume *Beyond Cop Cities: Dismantling State and Corporate-Funded Armies and Prisons.*[1] That book offers insights. Yet, as more conservative and reactionary politicians and authoritarians come into power—the rising militarism and mercenary presence within and beyond "democracy" have become normative. We note the two-party investment in genocides and militarism, multi-racial "leaders" funded by billionaires who seek to become trillionaires. We see that authoritarian governance means that "the whole damn system is guilty as hell." The duopoly of two parties is run by the ultra-wealthy and lobbyists. Supreme Court justices receive gifts and cash from billionaire reactionaries. Judges claim to revere the Constitution based in colonialism's archaic controls over laborers, impoverished, undocumented, children, women, men. Segments of all branches of government enable the state to menace and disappear the undocumented, nonbinary and trans people, racially stigmatized peoples, while imprisoning radicals and environmental protectors. The three-branched pitchfork of U.S. government—executive, legislative, and judicial—skewers spines and shreds fragile "safety nets."

U.S. domestic and foreign policies have subverted direct democracies and fostered occupations. Revitalizing colonial constructs eviscerates radical agency and civil/human rights, autonomy, and access for the mass to adequate shelter, food, housing, clean water, education and health care, and the legal right to protest and resist genocides and predatory wars. With *international* insights and organizing, the contributors to this book build conversations, critiques and confrontations to build on *Beyond Cop Cities* with bridges for discussions, debates, studies, strategies and confrontations. Following convicted felon Donald Trump's second inauguration as

President of the United States, *Confronting Counterinsurgency* critiques reactionary, conservative, liberal, and "radical" politics that monetize contemporary predatory warfare (leveraged by Project 2025 and other entities).[2] Mass deportations of ethical students and others protesting genocide and predatory warfare in Palestine and the Democratic Republic of the Congo enable the militarization of policing and the mercenary sacking of the resources of the people. Combating urban Cop Cities, this book addresses terrorism and abuse within prisons, environmental devastation, poverty, and colonizing domestic and foreign policies. It points to the global canopy of terror deployed against our lives and freedoms, and the loss of organizers and advocates for said freedoms.[3]

In 1951, the Civil Rights Congress (CRC), an all-Black unit in the Communist Party USA (CPUSA), issued an influential document created and edited by multiple intellectuals, including William Patterson and Paul Robeson. *We Charge Genocide: The Historic Petition to the United Nations for Relief from a Crime of the United States Government Against the Negro*[4] circulated throughout the globe after being presented to the United Nations by Black radical intellectuals and organizers. It placed the spectacle of genocide not solely on Nazis following the holocausts of World War II, by documenting U.S. complicity in genocidal violence shaped by the colonial and enslavement paradigms embedded in U.S. culture, government policies, and militarism.

This small book does not attempt to match the scope of *We Charge Genocide* or larger texts critiquing counterinsurgency. Yet, it reflects our commitments to analysis, resistance, and revolutionary love. In ten chapters, we document and describe the horrors perpetrated against national and international communities, and analyze strategies for confronting colonial, racial, gender and environmental violence. The agency and strategies of community protectors and war resisters is central to this text. *Confronting Counterinsurgency* seeks to examine U.S. predatory domestic and foreign policies, as well as confront those policies with an intellectual commitment to revolutionary love and resistance. We reject all violations fueled by: policing; militarism; trafficking and disappearance of humans and other animal species; devastation of wildlife, clean air, water, earth

2

and food; the mass incarcerations, deportations, imprisonment and torture at and beyond the borders and within U.S.-controlled territories. U.S.-American norms are rooted in imperialism, colonialism, reactionary religious fundamentalism, and deep hatred of Indigenous, Black, and racialized populations. Also vilified are politicized rebels, people with nonconforming genders, exploited laborers, unhoused, impoverished, and imprisoned individuals and communities.

Predatory domestic and foreign policies converge. Here, chapters address the U.S., Egypt, Puerto Rico, Palestine, Canada, Brazil, and the Congo, and grapple with 21st-century colonial or "settler states" and their historical and contemporary genocidal mandates. This small book is not comprehensive of every territory and site defending itself from conquest. However, it offers some strategies and wisdom about global freedom struggles.

Anti-colonial and anti-imperial freedom movements are intimately familiar with betrayal, death, and mourning. This book project is a study guide and a revolutionary manual shaped by the conversations and reflections and analyses of maroons. We care for each other, even when we do not agree, and we push ourselves forward to more deeply connect with liberation movements. We scrutinize our failures and flaws. We materialize and show up as caretakers, protesters, movement makers, maroon engineers, war resisters, and sanctuary stabilizers, seeking and demanding protections for all life forms. Reverence for the waters that carried us to various shores, and the tides that can alter our trajectories in freedom struggles. We are mindful of political prisoners who remain captives of the state, and note their reflections on violence and resistance. We also acknowledge the missteps, nondisclosure and confusions within our movements, for example the 1973 killing of civil rights activist Perry Ray Robinson at Wounded Knee,[5] on the Pine Ridge Indian Reservation in South Dakota.

In January 2025, President Joe Biden, departing from the White House, granted clemency to American Indian Movement (AIM) leader and political prisoner Leonard Peltier. Peltier was incarcerated for fifty years, gravely ill, framed by COINTELPRO, the infamous and nefarious FBI counter-intelligence program created under J. Edgar Hoover. The counter-intelligence program falsely implicated radical activists in crimes, and even at times orchestrated assassinations of Black revolutionaries, such as Chicago Black Panthers Fred Hampton and Mark Clark, for opposing white nationalism, capitalism, and imperialism. Potential political prisoners were and are disappeared, physically and/or geographically. Indigenous peoples in the Americas—such as AIM half a century ago—and international Indigenous people today—such as Mahmoud Khalil[6]— suffer(ed) and resist(ed) as political prisoners to educate those not yet captive.

Several months before he received clemency, Leonard Peltier shared with the public Peltier's Day of Mourning Statement, on November 24, 2024, the day of colonial "Thanksgiving":

> I am honored that you still hold me in your thoughts, believe in me, pray for me, and want to hear my words.
>
> It has been over 400 years since the settlers set out to civilize us. They began by taking our blood, our children, to Spain. We were the first slaves in this "great nation," built on stolen land, with stolen lives and stolen labor.
>
> The king and queen of Spain fell in love with our children and tried to end the slavery of American Indians. The colonizers used every loophole they could find. They did not want to give up the stolen labor of our people. They moved on to the stolen lives of our Black brothers and sisters, torn from their homelands.
>
> Our blood, our sweat, and our pain will forever bind us.[7]

Our small book(s)—*Beyond Cop Cities* and *Confronting Counterinsurgency*—are collectively written. We acknowledge that through the word and the resistance over centuries of blood and pain. We continue to seek to dismantle democracy's terrors: environmental devastations, enslavement, deportations, occupations, mass and political imprisonment, theft of labor and land, femicide, exploitation and harm of children, and genocide.

4

Anti-revolutionary Presidents of the United States (POTUSES)

President Donald Trump granted clemency to nearly 1,600 people who attacked the Capitol on January 6, 2021 at his behest, when he lost the November 2020 election to Joe Biden. Trump never referred to his followers as "terrorists" although some planned to assassinate Vice President Mike Pence to stop him from certifying the 2020 election and the transfer of power to Biden. Members of the Democratic Party did identify the insurrectionists as "terrorists," but since so many were granted clemency by POTUS Trump that label did not stick. So, what is the meaning of "counterinsurgency" in these times?

Those labeled "terrorists" by the state rarely include white nationalists, conservatives, or reactionaries or billionaire raiders of the public coffers. Likewise, POTUSES (and the CIA/FBI) are largely exonerated from the violence they foment to promote and stabilize colonialism, racism, and genocides. Counterinsurgency claims that it is fighting "counterterrorism" but the (Black) activists during Black Lives Matter's peak, the environmental protectors in the US and Amazon, those fighting to end the genocidal wars in Palestine, the Democratic Republic of the Congo, and Myanmar are likely surveilled and categorized as "counterinsurgents" and so become the enemies of the imperial state. Influenced by the Heritage Foundation Project 2025,[8] the state criminalizes the poor/working-class, racialized/Black, nonbinary, Muslim, antifascist, environmental protectors, and communities and nonconforming citizens and residents who are seeking their rights, equity and equality.

Counterinsurgency is a policing labyrinth; it annexes "counterterrorism" with "ecoterrorism." Shutting down a gas/oil pipeline or protesting toxic waste or defending oneself from militarized policing might be described by the (police) state as "terroristic"— but not obeying the police when they are inflicting harm or violating human rights and Constitutional rights does not make one a "terrorist" any more than condemning genocidal US foreign policies makes you a criminal. Exercising First Amendment speech rights and participating in protests have led to the state creating more political prisoners. In addition to long-term detainees as political

5

prisoners (for example Mumia Abu-Jamal and Rev. Joy Powell, as noted by Jericho),[9] mass protests took place against the imprisonment, torture and abuse of ethical people—also enduring political imprisonment were/are Mahmoud Khalil,[10] Mohsen Mahdawi (released April 30, 2025),[11] and Rumeysa Ozturk (released May 9, 2025).[12] After criticizing U.S. foreign policy for funding genocide, the state and some media vilified the three university graduate students as "terrorists"—arrested, detained, and incarcerated (two at a Louisiana ICE [Immigration, Customs and Enforcement agency] camp), and marked for removal from the U.S. despite their legal right to remain in the country.

Orwellian speech claims that environmental protectors are "ecoterrorists." *Yale Environment 360* reports that 2,000 environmentalists were assassinated in the last decade.[13] But the number of terrorized organizers killed prior to that remains unknown. For example, environmentalist Ken Saro-Wiwa,[14] who opposed SHELL and EXXON drilling for oil and polluting Ogoni lands, was executed in Nigeria in 1995; anti-Cop Cities environmentalist "Tortuguita" was executed in Georgia, USA in 2023. States and corporations arrest, torture, and execute environmentalists as "terrorists." The "counterinsurgency" functions to discredit, isolate, and liquidate the environmental protectors, those upholding workers' rights, trans activists, anti-racist organizers battling genocide, and protesters condemning rapes in the household or community, and in war zones by predatory armies.

POTUSES have not accurately explained their past, present, and future funding of terror and genocide. Historically, U.S. training of Latin American death squads at the "School of the Americas," Ft. Benning, GA, USA; or the CIA's destabilizations and assassinations of "Third World" leaders to provide U.S. corporations with the labor conditions they desire in the global South). After the World Trade Center was felled and the Pentagon struck on 9/11 (September 11, 2001), President George W. Bush's administration lied about "weapons of mass destruction" in Iraq and provoked a war that killed hundreds of thousands of people in Iraq and the Middle East. From those tragedies in the U.S. and the Middle East arose another: the Department of Homeland Security (DHS), which oversees

6

"counter-terrorism, border security, and Immigration, Customs and Enforcement (ICE) detentions. A decade later, President Barack Obama's administration authorized several drone assassinations in Yemen that killed at least three U.S.-born citizens. Cleric Anwar al-Awlaki had ties to Al-Qaeda and had condemned and threatened the U.S.; he was killed, without arrest or trial, with another U.S.-born man in Yemen in September 2011. Abdulrahman Anwar al-Awlaki, the sixteen-year-old son (born in Denver, Colorado) was assassinated by a U.S. drone strike, in October, two weeks after his father was killed. The teen was staying in another town in Yemen with his paternal grandfather, and preparing to return to high school in the U.S.

Joe Biden's funding of mass death in the Middle East was more striking. The Institute for Policy Studies reports that Biden and the US Congress funded genocidal violence against Palestinians, providing Israel with its annual $3.8 billion in U.S. military assistance in April 2024; Israel also received from Congress an additional $14.1 billion in military aid. Further U.S. support for the Israeli government war carnage, largely against civilians, "cost taxpayers at least another $4.86 billion."[15]

U.S. Americana state speech and performances are increasingly deadly and Orwellian. Constitutional rights, civil rights, and international human rights are suppressed by the state, and diluted by reactionary, conservative and centrist media. Trump cabinet members pose for "selfies" before half-dressed caged men/nonbinary people with shaven heads; some of them U.S. residents transported "as gang members" from the U.S. to El Salvador's CECOT (Terrorism Confinement Center [Centro de Confinamiento del Terrorismo]). In his April 2025 White House meeting, El Salvador president Nayib Bukele refused to return an American resident Kilmar Ábrego Garcia who was mistakenly sent to El Salvador's gulag prison. The POTUS "joked" in a meeting with Bukele that five more draconian prisons should be built in El Salvador to house (and terrorize) U.S. Americans, whom POTUS referred to as "homegrown criminals." When Bukele—the self-described stylish dictator— responded with the quip "We've got space," the Oval Office burst into laughter.

Book Structure

Part I, "Carceral Cities," moves past *Beyond Cop Cities* to link militarized policing to colonization. The first two chapters consist of analytical conversations that illuminate the predatory violence embedded in state policies. In Chapter 1, "Atlanta's Black Community Says 'Stop Cop Cities!'," Georgia organizer, educator and pastor Reverend Keyanna Jones Moore is interviewed by *BAR* (*Black Agenda Report*) Executive Editor Margaret Kimberley. In a 2025 email sent to this editor, Reverend Jones Moore reflected on her June 2023 interview with *BAR* and the necessity to organize leadership to stop the growth of Cop Cities [the Atlanta Police Training Center officially opened April 29, 2025, news reported its approximate cost at $116m, on the same day Georgia reporters noted that local Head Start programs for low-income young children were facing cuts due to limited public funding]:

> The impact of colonialism and its residual effects have recently come to the forefront of the national stage. Cop City has been a focal point for organizing against the same. Resistance to the inception of Cop City in Atlanta, Georgia was the flashpoint for so much of the protests against imperialism, fascism and colonialism. Thus, it is important to examine the conditions that led to the idea of "Cop Cities." It is equally important to understand the mental manipulation that is required for such an idea to be encouraged and widely accepted.... the effects of colonization on the minds of Black people in the so-called Black Mecca.... the Black Misleadership Class has been used as a tool of oppression and to perpetuate such a state of mind. Given Atlanta's place in history as the "cradle of the Civil Rights Movement," being the home of Rev. Dr. Martin Luther King, Jr., and the assumed bastion of his legacy, it bears acknowledging that Atlanta has an ugly truth behind its idyllic façade.

"Resisting [Global] Cop Cities and the Militarization of Policing," Chapter 2, transcribes a 2024 conversation with the Pluto Podcast "Radicals in Conversation," hosted by Chris Browne, who discusses with organizers Liliana, Kalonji Changa, and Joy James the colonial violence that ties Cop Cities to the School of the Americas and the de-stabilization and repression of Latin America. Chapter 3, "1492: Indigenous Sovereignty and Black Self-Determination," stems from a 2024 Black Power Media/Guerrilla Intellectual University interview with Mohamed Abdou and Ashanti Alston by Kalonji Changa and Joy James. Author of *Islam and Anarchism*,[16] Abdou leads a discussion on the de-stabilization and destruction of Indigenous communities in the 15th century when Columbus's invasion—funded by royalty in Spain and Portugal—led to the devastation of the Americas through genocide and enslavement that fueled the conquest of the continent and to this day enables repressive universities and colleges, and media, to deflect or deny predatory warfare and genocides. The chapter addresses spirituality, religion, conquest, and communities of resistance. Abdou (then a visiting professor at Columbia University) and Alston (a veteran of the Black Panther Party and Black Liberation Army) speak about assaults on student organizing and protests against genocide, their demands for a humanitarian ceasefire and a ban on war crimes against Palestinians. A number of university presidents and administrations, led by the state and donors, attacked peaceful protesters. In NYC, the NYPD brutalized students and some faculty, which was also true in California and other states. Speech for peace rather than war atrocities was criminalized. The violence against the youth, those attending elite and standard schools, was horrific, but that violence was surpassed by police terror used against working-class and largely racialized students in public universities such as City College in Harlem, located some twenty blocks north of Columbia University. Race and class, or racism and classism, rendered some peaceful protesters more vulnerable to state violation than others.

Part II, "Battling Colonialism," begins with Chapter 4, the 2024 statement by Benjamin Ramos to the United Nations Committee on Decolonization and Puerto Rico, in which Ramos denounces U.S. colonization and exploitation of the island. Chapter 5 reprints the November 28, 2024, Oxford Union Address by Palestinian author and poet susan abulhawa who posted her speech on X. It was later published by *The Massachusetts Review* editor(s) who describe the author's "historic address":

> On November 28, 2024, the Oxford Union debated the resolution: "This house believes that Israel is an apartheid state responsible for genocide."
>
> Israeli academic Gerald Steinberg, invited to oppose the motion, published a diatribe against the Oxford Union for considering such a debate. Israeli historian Benny Morris agreed to speak in opposition, then withdrew at the last moment. The opposing team threatened to cancel the debate unless they were allowed to add a fourth speaker, Mosab Hassan Yousef, a former Palestinian spy. The final team opposing the proposition consisted of UK Lawyers For Israel Charitable Trust legal director Natasha Hausdorff, writer and Oxford alum Jonathan Sacerdoti, former Palestinian spy Mosab Hassan Yousef, and CEO of Arab-Israeli NGO Together Vouch for Each Other, Yoseph Haddad. On the team supporting the motion, academic Norman Finkelstein also withdrew at the last minute. The president of the Oxford Union, Ebrahim Osman-Mowafy, stepped up to take his place. The rest of the supporting team was comprised of Palestinian writer and activist susan abulhawa, Palestinian poet and activist Mohammed El-Kurd, and anti-Zionist Israeli writer Miko Peled. Mohammed El-Kurd left the chamber immediately after giving his remarks, stating "It dishonors me to be in the same room as Mosab Hassan Yousef and Yoseph Haddad." Haddad's subsequent behavior led to his removal by security. The motion—"This house believes that Israel is an apartheid state responsible for genocide"—passed overwhelmingly by 278 to 59 votes.

The tragedies of war, invasions, occupations, exploitation and disappearances exist across the globe. In the Democratic Republic of the Congo (DRC), wars decimate a country and a people. In January 2025, Black Power Media interviewers Kalonji Changa and Rev. Keyanna Jones Moore hosted a roundtable discussion with organizers Maurice Carney, Brother Passy, Kwame Wilburg, Dr. Ikema Ojore, Claude Gatebuke. Transcribed and edited in Chapter

6, "Fighting for the Congo," the roundtable analyzes the invasions by Rwanda and Uganda, allegedly sponsored by the United States and Western powers, and the extreme—genocidal-level—violence in the Congo against civilians. The war atrocities and occupations remain largely under-scrutinized by the West.

Part III, "Counter Moves," looks at resistance. Chapter 7, "The Prisoner Human Rights Movement, 2025 Nobel Letter—and the Agency of PHRM," is based on a PHRM's organizing to further educate this editor on the work of incarcerated people advocating for anti-violence agency, nominated to the Nobel Committee. In Chapter 8, "The Abolition of Carceral Schooling," rosalind hampton analyzes school pedagogies that encourage or discourage intellectual radicalism and political agency for transformative education that resists colonial mandates.

The education of Black peoples targeted for imprisonment and premature death is analyzed in text excerpted from *Rise Up or Die!* (Common Notions). "Black (Brazilian) Futurity," Chapter 9, is based on dialogue with Brazilian organizers and educators Andréia Beatriz dos Santos, Hamilton Borges dos Santos, and joão costa vargas. *Rise Up or Die!* shares a radically intimate conversation between Black Brazilian resisters who reflect on systemic state violence and the urgency to protect communities of international or transnational resisters and revolutionary lovers. Weighing into systemic and unrelenting anti-black violence, their conversation grapples with rage and police attacks on favelas. Their insights and emphases on spirituality and futurity offer a zone that strengthens survivors and fighters.

This book's final chapter focuses on visuals created by artists kai barrow, Jazz Franklin, and Kara Lynch in Chapter 10, "When Opportunity Knocks ..." Here, barrow, Franklin, and Lynch provide a narrative for Black Geographies in resistance to social/political/police repression. Creating a hybrid visual collage/essay of abolitionist Black Geographies, counter-publics, and Blues epistemologies, this chapter provides, in an era of increasing monopolization of information and repression of radical speech, a study guide for creating mobile, autonomous communication units from recycled and donated equipment. Visuals are drawn from Radio Outlaw's

11

archive of documentation of community-led actions, trainings, and workshops, as well as planning notes, maps, drawings, and speculative collages. The study guide provides archives of maps, notes, diagrams, collages, drawings, and photo documentation from Radio Outlaw's communities and alliances shaped by Cooperation Gumbo, a project of Cooperation New Orleans. By broadcasting "Stories from the Marketplace" about cooperatives as a viable strategy for economic sustainability, Radio Outlaw disrupts capitalism, focusing on New Orleans communities and Black, BIPOC, LGBTQ, immigrant and migrant, underground and undocumented workers.

The editor's Conclusion, "Democracy's Terrors and Our Endless Resistance," focuses on: revolutionary legacies, counterinsurgencies and cooptation of revolutionary struggle, and the capacity of communities to leverage art, analyses, culture and care to resist endless wars.

PART I

CARCERAL CITIES

CHAPTER ONE

Atlanta's Black Community Says "Stop Cop Cities!"[1]

Rev. Keyanna Jones Moore interview by Margaret Kimberley BAR (Black Agenda Report)

Margaret Kimberley: Reverend Keyanna Jones is an Atlanta-based minister and an organizer with Community Movement Builders. She joins us to discuss the movement to Stop Cop City, the Atlanta Public Safety Training Center. You know, the last week has been a very interesting time there in Atlanta, around Stop Cop City activities. The first thing we can talk about is the Atlanta Solidarity Fund. Tell our listeners about the Atlanta Solidarity Fund and about their arrest.

Reverend Keyanna Jones Moore: The Atlanta Solidarity Fund operates as a faction of a nonprofit organization that exists to ensure that as people are exercising their First Amendment right to protest and express dissent, that in the event that they are arrested for any reason, the Atlanta Solidarity Fund will provide bail and bond assistance. They will also help with legal representation, so that people are not discouraged from exercising their First Amendment right to protest. The arrests (in 2023) were shocking, to say the least. There had been discussion about the domestic terrorism charges levied against protesters, and there had been word of possible RICO* charges against people who were working within the movement together to help people with bail, to help people with legal representation, and just RICO charges and domestic terrorism charges against people within the movement in general. So,

---

* RICO refers to the Racketeer Influenced and Corrupt Organizations Act.

while it was not a surprise that it happened … that everyone in this movement is now a target. It was still very shocking … [for the state] to charge this Solidarity Fund with charity fraud and money laundering simply because people are being reimbursed for gas and mileage and the supplies that they've purchased for the bail fund. It shows overreach … desperation, and that there is no limit to what Mayor Andre Dickens, his administration, and the Atlanta Police Foundation will do to try to make sure that Cop City goes forward.

Kimberley: Those three individuals were arrested by a SWAT* team, cops in military gear, the Georgia Bureau of Investigation and Atlanta cops. It was the kind of thing that you see if someone has a bomb or hostages, [or made a] violent threat. These extraordinary measures were taken for what are very dubious charges. Was that not shocking to see a SWAT team arresting these people?

Jones: That is absolutely the part that was shocking. I have never in all of my years, and I am 43 years old so I've seen a lot in my time, seen anyone arrested on fraud charges or money laundering charges, be met with a SWAT team that would come to the home to serve a warrant. SWAT has never been in the mix for so-called white-collar crimes. It's really alarming that SWAT showed up for these particular individuals who are part of a bail fund that has been helping protesters against Cop City, which is such a hot button issue here in the city of Atlanta and in the nation honestly. People who are against Cop City have been targeted simply for dissent. The domestic terrorism charges that are being levied are the first ever to be levied in the state of Georgia under that law, which was passed in 2017. This is really alarming. We saw that there was a SWAT team. That this was overkill. There's absolutely no reason for a SWAT team to go in and retrieve three people who you were arresting for money laundering and charity fraud.†

Kimberley: What has the commentary been about these very flimsy charges from leadership in Atlanta, from the media? I know that

---

* Special Weapons and Tactics
† The three individuals were jailed and released on bond.

the political class, the media, have all been in favor of Cop City. Have any of them registered any opposition, any protest, to what happened?

Jones: Governor Brian Kemp, of Georgia, released a statement saying that the arrest of those individuals was a victory for the state of Georgia, because it shows Georgia's commitment against terrorism. And that Georgia won't stand for terrorism within its borders, and that the state of Georgia and Attorney General Chris Carr won't rest until each and every one of them who has any part of this, or any part in this, is arrested. That was Governor Kemp's victory lap, and Mayor Andre Dickens, of course, wanted to ride along with that. But what we saw with the arrest of the three individuals connected with the bail fund—representatives in the Georgia General Assembly who had not previously made any comment about Cop City or the protests ... came out and spoke against the way the raid was conducted, because it was literally a raid with SWAT and the Georgia Bureau of Investigation [GBI]. They did express concern with the raid, what the people were being charged with, and how it was conducted.

Kimberley: Georgia U.S. Senator Jon Ossoff stated in his tweet: "proponents and opponents of the proposed Atlanta Police Training Center continue to engage in vigorous advocacy; while most advocacy has been peaceful, an extremist minority has engaged in violence that cannot be tolerated." I responded, "only the cops killed anyone, so I guess you're referring to them." So that was my snarky remark. But who else has been violent in the protests against Cop City, other than the police?

Jones: It is really funny that politicians and police officers believe that property damage is violence. So what they commonly refer to is an incident that took place during the last week of action on March 5, where some construction equipment was set afire. What I will say is that I am in total agreement with you. There has been no one who has exacted violence in this movement and during this time other than police, because we have seen them not only brutalize people, but they murdered Manuel Esteban Paez Terān, known as Tortuguita, as they sat with their hands up, cross-legged in meditation. They were executed with 57 bullet wounds, in what the GBI claimed was self-defense, because they claimed that Tortuguita fired at an officer first. But there has been body-cam footage that was released and quickly taken away, that suggests that the officer who was shot, was shot by friendly fire from another officer. We know now, because of an independent autopsy and an official autopsy, that Tortuguita did not shoot at officers first, there was not even gunpowder residue found on their hands. And what's more important, because some people will say, "Oh well, they followed up and said that there was a gunpowder-like substance that was found on their hands, there were traces of that." When your body is riddled with 57 bullets, and many of those bullets go into your hands because they are raised, yeah, there could be traces of gunpowder residue from the bullets that hit you from a police officer's gun. So, there have been no members of our movement who have exacted violence on other people, but the police serve property over people, as we have seen, so they classify property destruction or property damage as violence.

Kimberley: The autopsy of Tortuguita showed 57 bullet wounds. But we get these admonishments from Senator Ossoff about violent protest. Cop City hasn't even opened, and somebody has already been killed by the police. That explains why there is so much community opposition to it.

Jones: The tactics that we are seeing employed against protesters of Cop City, are some of the same tactics that were used against Dr King and many leaders in the Civil Rights Movement. When you talk about protesters and protests needing to be peaceful, what we saw in the days of the Civil Rights Movement was people simply sitting at a lunch counter brutalized by others and then further brutalized by police officers. You saw people peacefully marching in the streets with water hoses and dogs turned on them by police. And here again, you see us doing some of the same things last night, or rather this morning, when the council finally voted to continue funding for Cop City. There were people who were angry, there were people who were hurt, there were people who raised their voices, they called the council members cowards, they called them some other expletives, all of which is protected by the First Amendment. But not one of those people raised a hand in violence toward a council person. Yet we were met in City Hall yesterday with officers in riot gear. The number of officers was astronomical. With what they have been calling a crime wave in the city of Atlanta, I don't understand how they could have afforded to spare so many officers to be in one place at one time. Those same officers showed up in riot gear, with rifles, with helmets, dressed as if they are ready for battle with the people, and it reminded me of the same way those officers marched the streets during the Civil Rights Movement to brutalize our ancestors.

Kimberley: You made reference to the city council vote. Now, before the city council voted to approve funding, it was revealed that the cost of Cop City is twice as much as the public were first told. Initially it was $30 million. Atlanta will spend more than $60 million. The city council vote was eleven to four, to approve continued funding. What does this tell us about politics in Atlanta?

Jones: It definitely tells us that politics in Atlanta is the same as many of us know, that is the "Atlanta way." Because when we talk about the cost of this project, and the public finding out that the cost would double, be very clear that the council members found out that the cost would double at the same time that the public did. However, those council members who are so weak and so desperate to have the approval of Mayor Andre Dickens and the so-called Black elite in Atlanta, they decided that they would rather bankrupt the people of Atlanta then go against the mayor.

And that has truly been the Atlanta way, because the mayor is having his strings pulled by the APF,* which is run by greedy corporations. So here we have racialized capitalism at work as it has been in the city of Atlanta for so many decades. The Black ruling class of Atlanta have this partnership with the white supremacist

---

* Atlanta Police Foundation.

infrastructure where they keep the rest of us Negroes under control, and keep us in our places in exchange for status and a place at the table where they believe they are going to enjoy political promotion and then they can be a part of an inner circle of wealth and status in the city of Atlanta. That is exactly what we saw happen with that vote.

Kimberley: Why is there a drive to get this "public safety training center" built in the middle of a beautiful old-growth forest … destroyed in order to build this training center, as if police have no place to train in Atlanta?

Jones: For whatever reason, Mayor Andre Dickens is lending himself to white supremacy and engaging in environmental racism. I have no idea what it is that he is being threatened with or incentivized with to do this. Neither Mayor Andre Dickens, the Atlanta Police Foundation, nor council members who voted to ram this project through care about Black people in the city of Atlanta.

That neighborhood is the neighborhood where I was born and raised, where my granny still lives, where I lived until a month ago. That neighborhood, the Blackest neighborhood in southeast Atlanta that has not yet been hit heavily by gentrification, that has two schools right outside of that forest, where they are willing to have a burn tower to further pollute the air that our children breathe, where they already have a firing range where the air is continually polluted with noise from bullets constantly flying. Those same bullets go into the wastewater treatment facility right there by the facility, and that lead runs off into our water. They are going to cut down 381 acres of trees in a Black neighborhood that has already been the victim of environmental racism for decades. There are still landfills in that neighborhood that are now closed, but still there. We are still breathing in that pollution. We are still drinking that crap that goes into our water. [When] you're not willing to put [a Cop City] in a place like Buckhead, or anywhere in North Fulton County [which includes the city of Atlanta] because it's heavily populated by white people, you are showing me that this is environmental racism.

Kimberley: Atlanta has this reputation as being a Mecca for Black people. Those of us in the rest of the country are told Atlanta is a place "that's good for Black people," where Black people thrive, where you have Black political leadership, and a large professional class. Yet, the Cop City project and the protest tell us that that image is a false one.

Jones: Atlanta boasts the highest, largest wealth gap in this country, the wealth gap between its white citizens and its Black citizens is the highest in this country. Don't tell me that you're the Black Mecca, but Black people are struggling for adequate housing and sufficient nutrition and equal opportunities to employment. Black people are struggling to get their businesses off the ground. Black people are struggling to not be harassed by police in Atlanta. Don't tell me that this is a "Black Mecca." This is not what a Black Mecca looks like.

The training at Cop City is not de-escalation training. This facility will be a MOUT city—"Military Operations on Urban Terrain"—built for urban warfare training. That is in the description of that project. The Atlanta Police Foundation, Mayor Andre Dickens and the city of Atlanta are building this Cop City so that they can train in warfare on Black bodies.

CHAPTER TWO

Resisting [Global] Cop Cities and the Militarization of Policing

Liliana, Joy James, Kalonji Changa, interview by Chris Browne[1]

Chris Browne: What happens when the police become an army? Since 1997, the U.S. Department of Defense [DOD] has transferred more than $7.2 billion in military equipment to law enforcement agencies. The DOD is legally required to make various items and equipment available to local police and school police departments, from flashlights and sandbags to grenade launchers and armored vehicles.

This militarization has, unsurprisingly, been shown to unjustly impact on Black communities and is associated with increasing killings by police. The Police Public Safety Training Center in Atlanta, more commonly known as Cop City, is just the latest manifestation of the militarization of policing. It's a costly and controversial endeavor being rammed through by the local Democrat-run administration in the face of fierce, widespread opposition among local communities.

Resistance to the project has been met with spurious legal roadblocks, activist intimidation and violent repression. One environmental activist known as Tortuguita, was killed by Atlanta state troopers, shot repeatedly while they sat with their hands raised and their legs crossed. But Cop City is far from being just a local issue. Almost every U.S. state now has a Cop City project of their own in some stage of development. The logic, structures, and ramifications of Cop Cities are truly international. It's a real honor to be joined on the show today by three people who are deeply connected to the Stop Cop City movement, Liliana, Joy James, and Kalonji Changa.

Liliana, Joy, Kalonji, and I discuss the history of the Public Safety Training Center in Atlanta; the links between U.S. law enforcement and the Israeli police; the parallels between Cop Cities and the notorious School of the Americas; and the ways in which the tactics and logic of U.S. imperialism abroad, particularly in relation to Latin America, are being brought to bear on working-class and racialized communities at home. We discuss Cop Cities and the book *Beyond Cop Cities: Dismantling State and Corporate-Funded Armies and Prisons....* [2] What does the phrase "Cop Cities" refer to?

Kalonji Changa: Cop Cities. It's supposed to be the Atlanta Public Safety Training Center, and it's commonly known as Cop City, renamed by a number of different activists, forest defenders: the activists here, primarily in the Atlanta area. It was started under the guise of being a police and fire department training campus, which is under construction in what is originally known as the Weelaunee Forest, [renamed by the state as] South River Forest. It's in Dekalb County Atlanta. This area, the city leased the 381 acres of it, is basically stolen land, stolen Muskogee land from the Muskogee people. They lived there until about the 1830s, and the U.S. federal government forced them off that land and into what is known as Oklahoma, during the Trail of Tears. Later, it was purchased by the city of Atlanta, I believe in around 1867 or so, and it became a prison farm. And there's been all types of different situations that have taken place on that particular land. But to fast forward and make it as basic as possible, it is a space in which the city of Atlanta, along with the police unions here, had been plotting and planning for probably a good twenty years. In September of 2021, Atlanta Mayor Keisha Lance Bottoms, along with Dave Wilkinson, who was the CEO of the Atlanta Police Foundation, decided that this site would be selected to house this particular training center. Folks who understand police state and understand imperialism see it as a paramilitary training compound where occupier forces receive instruction in preparedness on domestic urban warfare.

We understand this as an extension of the police state and as corporate funded. Millions of dollars, we're talking about $90 million plus at this time, has been allocated and delivered by a number of different corporations, including Amazon, UPS, JP Morgan, Coca-Cola, Chick-Fil-A, Microsoft and many others. So, they're looking at 85 acres of this former slave plantation turned city prison farm.

They're looking at taking this to pretty much maintain hegemony and to continue the rise of a fascist state under the guise of proper training. We know that here in the United States, over 1,500 people are murdered by police yearly. So, you know, we're not quite sure what type of training they would receive other than maintaining what's already been established.

Joy James: When I think about "Cop Cities," I see concentric circles. There's the city that Kalonji's talking about—Atlanta, Georgia. It's been the marquee flashing "We Are Cop City."* There might be 70+ urban centers creating Cop Cities facilities. In New York City, Mayor Eric Adams is raising money for a "Cop City" in Queens, New York.†

Cop Cities is ... a national attempt to make militarized policing the norm. Kalonji mentioned 2021 and Keisha Lance Bottoms. That former city mayor of Atlanta supported Cop Cities and then moved to Washington DC to become one of the senior advisors to the POTUS Joe Biden.‡

I think of 2021, one year after George Floyd was killed. Knee on the neck. A horrific way to die. People yelling at the curb for Derek Chauvin/police to release him. Taking cell photos is not a [sufficient] strategy to deal with police brutality and police murders. But 2020 was the height globally [of protests against predatory policing]. In the UK and around the globe, people protested police violence. In 2024, under a Democratic administration, police have received more state money and killed more civilians....

Cop Cities is part of U.S. foreign policy, domestic policy, urban or city policy.... We have to think about the convergence of control [and its] worst impact on people who are working-class, Indigenous,

---

* The Atlanta city mayor and city council broke ground for the facility at the end of April 2025.
† Adams, whose felony charges were dropped by Trump, allows ICE to raid sites for undocumented people in NYC, which is a "sanctuary city."
‡ President Biden gave tens of billions of dollars to U.S. policing.

Black, urban, impoverished, those without wealth or protections from a government that is not functioning in their interests.

Browne: Thanks, Joy. As you say, [this is] definitely not a local issue to Atlanta. I think the isyourlifebetter.net website has an interactive map showing Cop Cities projects across the U.S., in varying stages of development. Seemingly only three states do not currently or are not currently pursuing their own Cop City. So, there's an alarming proliferation. [We are] talking about Atlanta, although of course, we know the opposition to Cop Cities is kind of beyond that. We're recording this on 30 September [2024]. Hurricane Helene has just caused all this devastation in parts of the south of America, including in Georgia. There's been lots of flooding.

And so, there's a political choice to spend whatever the figure was, you know, these tens of millions of dollars on pursuing this Cop City when that money is clearly needed in order to respond to things like extreme weather events as part of this ramping climate crisis. There's a choice there that goes kind of fundamentally against what people want. Could you speak, Kalonji, a little bit to the local opposition or the local feeling? I mean, there has been a lot of opposition, hasn't there?

Changa: Oh yeah, absolutely, in Atlanta. And we appreciate you pointing out the whole Hurricane Helene. It's just wreaked havoc. You know 4.4 million people lost power between Florida, Georgia, South Carolina and North Carolina. Also, there was a chemical plant explosion right outside of Atlanta yesterday [September 2024].… The homeless population is at an all-time high. Folks lack medical care, adequate food, so on and so forth. There's a possible longshoreman strike. There's a lot, as you mentioned, going on. But indeed, the people as a whole have had strong opposition against this whole Cop City situation because, particularly, to be quite honest, folks in the Black community, many of them haven't quite shown up to some of the protests in spaces because of the fact that it's been business as usual.

If you're already being beaten, you're already being attacked, you're already being falsely arrested and accused, so on and so forth, it almost appears hopeless in many cases. But those who have organized on the ground, many who have great intent, while, being honest, others have come in and then made names for themselves for nonprofit purposes, to really get more resources and to gain notoriety and publicity.

It's a sad situation of sorts because, at the same time, you have RICO charges being launched against a number of different activists for quote unquote, funding, as little as $2 and some change for a roll of tape. The government has cracked down really hard. They've been giving a lot of push back. And we talk about RICO charges, of course, we talk about the Racketeer Influenced and Corrupt Organizations Act, which was primarily set up for the Mafia and organized crime.

But here we have 61 protesters indicted, charged for really nothing more than opposing militarized policing, opposing imperialism on a local level. You know, and as Joy pointed out, indeed Cop Cities, it is national, but I'm sure Liliana would take it even further and talk about how it's international. And I think one of the issues we have here in this particular conundrum is that even the activists here in Atlanta, many of them have looked at it as local, although they're seeing now, as it's been pointed out, you know, the national piece.

But, you know, it goes so much further. And we can tie this from Atlanta to Palestine without interruption because of some of the players that are involved. When we talk about Cop City, we're also talking about GILEE, which is a Georgia International Law Enforcement Exchange, which is an exchange between Israeli soldiers and Atlanta police, which has been going on for the past 31 years. But I'll stop there and let …

James: That's such an important bridge. The *Beyond Cop Cities* introduction quotes in a citation from *Jewish Voice for Peace*: 'For decades, the IDF* has trained with U.S. police, sheriffs, border control and FBI agents.' Right. And you can find that citation. It was published March 17, 2022. Given that everything's interlocked … how do we struggle?

---

* Israeli Defense Forces, also called the IOF—Israeli Occupation Forces—by Palestinians.

We approach this occupation as fragmented. Folks focus on different sectors. [It's more than] one city or "multiple cities." When we talk about MOUT* or the School of the Americas in Fort Benning, Georgia (known as "School of the Assassins" by pacifists and human rights advocates; people who want to end war and torture) we collectively need to deal with the fact that we're highly frightened and intimidated by the aggression of the police and their qualified immunity, or their ability to harm and kill people and still walk. We also have to think about federal policies and foreign policies. This is why what Liliana can share is so vital.

Liliana: Thank you for having me. I'm so grateful for this. So grateful for Joy and Kalonji. This book has opened the door to so many talks that people haven't talked about in so many years. Cop City is not 'Cop City', it's Cop Cities. It is not a local issue, it's an international issue.

Just like I keep saying, immigration is not a Mexican issue; it's way more than that. So again, I'm so grateful, this book opens the door to a lot of talks. I cannot talk about Cop Cities without talking about School of Americas. That's the first thing that came to my mind when I learned about Cop Cities. I was shaken for a minute and I was surprised at being surprised.

There has to be a Cop City everywhere in the U.S. Historically, the U.S. has always viewed Latin America as an open market, as a cheap labor and natural resource. That's all we are for the United States. Most of the time they don't even know where we are, where are our communities, if we speak any other language besides Spanish. They don't know anything about culture, but they do know about resources: we are an open market for the U.S. The fear of the U.S. losing this control, losing these open markets has taken them to coups d'état, death squads, all kinds of crimes against our communities in fear of losing that control. And really the U.S. doesn't see their own citizens much different as the way they see Latin America. The same way the U.S. sees Latin America, the same way the U.S. sees Black communities, immigrant communities, and poor

---

* Military Operations on Urban Terrain

people in general. The School of the Americas (SOA) has been the most powerful tool that the U.S. has against our communities.

SOA has been the tool used for coups d'état and death squads. We don't even know how many people graduate from the School of the Americas. They've been able to keep it very secret. We have an idea, maybe 100,000 students, but we don't really know. SOA has been open [since 1946]. It started in Panama, [training] dictators, police officers, military. Those trained at the School of the Americas have been implicated in every single major crime in Latin America—massacres, coups d'état. Any big [atrocity]—if you dig in—was either by someone trained at the School of Americas or someone who trained with people that were trained in the School of the Americas. Massacres in Latin America, Central America are connected to the School of the Americas, from the Banana Massacre in 1928 in Colombia,* and the thousands of people were killed that were on strike. Who were the soldiers who committed these crimes? We don't have to go too far. In 1981 in El Salvador a whole village was wiped off the map, over a thousand people were killed in three days.[3] Most of them were children or women. Who was the soldier in charge of this? Monterrosa. Where was he trained? School of the Americas. Every major crime in Latin America, if you dig in, takes you back to the School of the Americas one way or another. Why is there secrecy with the School of the Americas? The same thing with Cop City. It's all connected. The same people they're going to train, these officers in Atlanta, are the same people training in the School of the Americas. The same people that killed people in these little villages in El Salvador, are the same people that are going to kill our students that are rallying in the streets against the genocide. It's all connected. In Colombia, in 1999, we had this agreement signed by U.S. President Bill Clinton and the Colombian government for a package of financial aid to Colombia to help the Colombian government to combat the drug trafficking.

It was a package of [$1.9 billion for 1999–2000 according to January 11, 2000, U.S. State Department website]. It was a lot of

---

* The massacre was of workers at the United Fruit Company, now known as "Chiquita."

money [for "Plan Colombia" which was to stop drug trafficking and equip the Colombian army to defeat rebels]. What was that money used for? Death squads trained by soldiers that went to School of the Americas. We had a hundred people disappear. We have mass graves all over the country.

Colombian rivers are mass graves. That's what the rivers are. Yeah, the waters are very pretty. The mountains are very pretty. But if you go and you talk to the people, if you go to the little villages, they tell you the rivers are mass graves. This money from the USA was used to finance all of these killings. We had a political party completely wiped out. It was a genocide.

The UP [the Patriotic Union]—[lost] over 7,000 people [who] were killed because they were part of the opposition, a leftist group. In 2010, there was a mass grave with 2,000 bodies. It was found right behind a military base. The government was questioned about it, the reason they gave for mass death was that … all of them were guerrillas. Well, even guerrillas need to go through prosecutions, trials, the courts You don't kill people just like that, and throw them in a mass grave. Most of the people in the mass graves, those 2,000 bodies were farmers, Indigenous people, Afro-Colombians and people working in their communities trying to just keep up with their land.

But we had these military groups going all over this little village. The government knows; of course, they know what's happening. They pay for this. Plan Colombia finances all of these groups and all of these people, again, if you dig in, were trained at the School of the Americas or they were trained by people that trained in the School of the Americas. I think SOA and Cop Cities is everywhere in the world. These soldiers, when they go to a little village, a little community, they bring all that knowledge from the School of the Americas. All of the soldiers, and many of the police officers, they did not go to the School of the Americas, because the school isn't that big; but they had the same knowledge from the people that trained there.

So, they bring that SOA or Cop Cities with them everywhere they go. We have right now coups d'état taking place; now, when we're talking, the president of Colombia has been sending emails.

29

He's been pretty much crying. There is a coup d'état taking place any time. We know it's happening. It almost happened not long ago in Venezuela, happened a few years ago in Bolivia. It's been happening all over the place. And again, when you dig in, who are the soldiers? Where did they train or who trained them? People talk about the School of the Americas like it's something from the past, something from 20–30 years ago. It's very relevant right now. It's very strong and it's even more dangerous because they've been able to keep it very secret.

Years ago, you were able to find a lot of information about SOA. You don't find that much information any more. We don't know who's really the graduates. We have a few names, but we don't have every single name. One of the most bloody coups d'état took place in Chile years ago.[4] Even now we don't know for sure if Augusto Pinochet went to the School of the Americas. There are a lot of rumors. We know for sure that his picture is mentioned as somewhere in the building. And they have this name, you know, someone very respected with a lot of honor, but we don't really know where he went. They've been able to keep a lot of names in secret, back then, and they're doing it now.

Beyond Cop Cities opened the door again to talk about these things as connected. We are having a huge immigration issue and a lot of the immigration agents were trained in School of the Americas. In the last seven years, a hundred people have been killed by immigration agents. Most of the immigrants, undocumented immigrants, don't report crime; they don't report rapes. They don't report being beat up. And about these agents, there's evidence of them going to Mexican territories and doing all these killings. A lot of these killings and crimes have never been reported. The undocumented community is very vulnerable and they're afraid. Most of the crimes committed by these immigration agents are never reported.

And, you don't have to kill someone to destroy them or to destroy their family. The large amounts of rapes are crazy. We have a mass grave in Falfurrias,[5] it's about a hundred miles from the border and is in the U.S. They just found a mass grave of people in the desert near the Mexican border, or the U.S. These bodies were thrown in a mass grave without any protocol. When these authorities find bodies in the desert, they assume they're going to be an undocumented immigrant. So that body doesn't mean anything; it's like a dog. They don't even check if they have any ID. They don't save the clothes. They don't take pictures like they're supposed to do. They just throw them in a mass grave.

The main thing is the amount of impunity. They get away with so much. How can you have a mass grave and [say you] just found it in the desert and [someone unknown just] threw [bodies] over there. That's not how it is supposed to work. This is happening because they get away with these things. I've said before: the way the U.S. views Latin America is pretty much the way they view poor communities, the Black community. With Central and Latin America and the immigrant community, the only difference is they can get away with a little more; the feeling is the same.

Browne: Thanks, Liliana. That's really enlightening. You see the logic of colonialism being practiced domestically through this kind of policing. We know that the history of foreign policy strategies being deployed in domestic policing is very long, almost from the inception of policing in the mid-19th century. Joy or Kalonji, would you like to pick up on what you were saying about how people in power view the working-class people of color in these communities, the same way as they view ordinary people in Latin America?

Changa: Thank you, Liliana. Oftentimes places like Latin America are regions that are overlooked, much like a number of different inner-city neighborhoods throughout the United States. There's been reports of murders inside of places like Chicago, New York, Connecticut, different places. You know, me growing up in Connecticut, I could just remember police corruption at an early age.

That cops brought drugs into the community was well known. Cops would take drugs from one particular [housing] project or bring it to another. And forcing youth to sell. This isn't something I saw on TV or heard about. This was going on in my neighborhood and we knew which cops would take you and bang your head up against the wall. We would get attacked by police so much that I wouldn't even tell my parents because I wanted to go outside. If I told them what was going on, I wouldn't be able to hang out and go with my friends. [Assaulting] 13-, 14-year-olds, cops were throwing folks on the ground.

Immigrants are also vulnerable, as Liliana mentioned; foolish Americans think of only Mexicans when discussing immigration. Concerning ICE [Immigration and Customs Enforcement] and immigration, the Haitian population has been under heavy attack.* When we talk about these ICE facilities, you know, you can find a lot of others. Besides, quote unquote, with these clowns, they talk about building a wall. There's been instances in certain neighborhoods where police have literally stuck screwdrivers up the anus of individuals, talking about they were looking for drugs, you know, doing all types of things.

To talk about policing on an international level, you must look at the U.S. military and its over 900 bases that exist across the planet. No country can set up shop outside of the U.S. or pretty much in the Western Hemisphere. However, the U.S. has domain, dominion. Israel and the U.S. The U.S. is 5% of the world population, controlling 25% of all resources ... and housing over 25% of all prisoners on the planet, but yet they reign supreme and hold dominion over the globe. They can set up shop wherever they want to, and when they can't get their way, they will set up these proxy wars that will get folks like the Ukrainians in a jam.

The U.S. wants to control these resources. We have this false sense of patriotic love for our nation and so on and so forth. When the reality is, the policing, home and abroad, is literally to maintain the gangs. And we talk about the gangs being the "founding fathers" who stole this land, who murdered [Indigenous and African] people. Look at the Weelaunee Forest alone ... the site for Georgia's Cop City. A place where settlers massacred and ran off natives of that particular land, the original victims of gentrification here in the United States. Then they turned it into [a plantation, and later a] prison farm. Now they want to turn it into essentially the local establish-

---

* See 2024 Trump presidential smear campaigns that Haitians are eating pets or 2016 Trump administration referencing African nations as "s**t-hole" countries.

ment of the military. They want to turn it into a base so they can play cops and robbers.

These corporations are funding it. They're in cahoots because they benefit from it. At the end of the day, it's all about capitalism, it's all about imperialism. And people will suffer. And as Liliana pointed out, yes, there'll be more coups. Why are there coups? Because it's about domination. It's about control, it's about debt. It's about keeping folks in servitude. So, at the end of the day, it's collateral damage.

James: On Pluto's website, there is a question which echoes what Liliana and Kalonji have put on the table: "What happens when the police become an army?" From that question another logically follows: "How do we resist an army?" There are different kinds of occupations and death squads, and contradictions. We're still grappling to comprehend that this [democracy has worked like] an army. As Kalonji says, first it [the "Cop City" land taken by the state] was Indigenous land; then a [white-owned] plantation; then it's a prison farm, and now it's the training site for lethal policing. [This is a zone] for predatory behavior against all lives, not just civilian, two-legged people or those in a wheelchair. Not just human life is taken in building a "Cop City." In taking over that territory, [police powers] poisoned the water, and the land.

No environmental organization [has been able to] collect the data on these forms of destruction. Once you start this kind of militarized presence, you poison the air. [The sounds of shooting and explosives will] negatively impact Black working families. So, we need clean air, clean water, clean land. Kalonji spoke earlier about the storms and hurricanes. Organizing [that confronts] the reality of varied occupations and militarized aggression will take us out of the liberal zone. We were trying to do [that] in *Beyond Cop Cities*.* The fairytale [is] that you could vote your way out of an occupation.

Acknowledge the structured violence against communities, against all populations seeking healthy autonomy. When people frame this struggle into a narrow corridor aligned with conventional

---

* We translated chapters of that book into Spanish and Portuguese.

liberal politics, we're … changing the narrative of this struggle: … you cannot fix this without having a major confrontation with all predatory acts by the state.

This is personal for all of us. We're compromised. All our communities are compromised. This definitely has a heavy impact on Indigenous, working-class, poor people, undocumented people. But there are people who are Black mayors, Black cops, Black military running the Pentagon, or Black women in leadership who refused to allow a call for a ceasefire in Palestine.* Decades ago, racial solidarity would say that we're on the outside and [all of us are] oppressed. Now, there are so many compradors, we have to let go of sentimental affiliations based on what we look like in order to focus increasingly on what war resistance is.

Browne: Thanks, Joy. That speaks to the chapter in *Beyond Cop Cities* by Atlanta-based Reverend Matthew V. Johnson who says that Atlanta is the "Blackest" city in America, you know, with a Black leadership class. And yet it also has the largest racial income disparity in the country. And you really kind of get the sense that the limits of electoralism as a political strategy are being felt there. Haven't there been something like 116,000 signatures delivered for this public referendum to put the brakes on it? And yet every sort of cynical legal challenge has been kind of thrown in the face of that, the kind of intimidation of the Atlanta Solidarity Fund. Those charges [were recently] dropped. This also puts me in mind of Peter Gelderloos, *They Will Beat the Memory Out of Us: Forcing Nonviolence on Forgetful Movements.*†

When there is this sort of asymmetry of power, as you say, when you're trying to resist and organize against militarized aggression, there has nevertheless been this kind of insistence on nonviolence as an organizing principle. What would you say to that? Do we need to move beyond nonviolence as a sort of matter of principle?

---

*   This was Linda Thomas-Greenfield, U.S. Ambassador to the UN.
†   Published by Pluto Press.

James: The language that I use is "war resistance." I don't want to get caught between "Are you for or against [war] …?" We've also talked about the language of "revolutionary love." Black Power Media (BPM) contributed to *Beyond Cop Cities*, a transcript of its 2024 "Attempted Assassinations against Mumia Abu-Jamal, Political Prisoner." Also, Kalonji and BPM worked on Marcellus Williams's death row case. Marcellus Williams was executed by the state of Missouri. There are other executions. There are different ways to kill people in the U.S. It's a comprehensive struggle. We're still fighting for the narrative of clarity because people are often painting [struggle] as something else—as conventional politics.

Conventional politics helped to create the war zone, because it's empire and colonialism. When we say *Beyond Cop Cities*, we're also talking about the prisons. Incarcerated author Kevin Rashid Johnson writes about how gangs were organized by wardens and guards. Violence in our communities is not always internal. External factors and actors come into the communities, bringing violence, drugs, guns, etc. [We can] move beyond fairytale narratives of comfort, like bedtime stories for your five-year-old to reassure them.

I think the issue of clarity and accepting the reality of a war machine is the first line of self-defense. What you do later in terms of security apparatuses becomes something else and sometimes private to your community.

Changa: We have to look at all victims of genocide. We have to look at all victims of police terrorism as actual family members. I think that the way propaganda works and the way we have been desensitized, it has us as Malcolm X would talk about, being lulled to sleep.

It's like we're breathing Novocaine … as the young folks would say, "It don't hit the same, when you don't feel that pain." The fact is we are numb, numbed by so many different distractions, everything from a phony electoral process that would have us arguing over, pardon my English, "bullshit." We are arguing about whether the warmonger Kamala Harris or the convicted felon should be president, when in fact it's like arguing over whether you want to worship Lucifer or Satan. I don't know about changing our strategies as far as from nonviolent to violent. I know that there's no preparation for any of that. But I do know that self-defense is not a violent act. And I do know that until we decide to be organized and almost go on strike as a people and say, this is not what we signed up for, we will not pay you to brutalize us, we will not pay you to terrorize us. We'll not pay taxes for you to treat us worse than animals. I would never advocate violence, but I would certainly support self-defense. I don't think anyone should be a victim. I don't think anyone should have to live their lives under tyranny and oppression and not at least, at the very least be vocal about it.

We live in a nightmare while believing that we have some type of dream that we can manifest. So again, to answer your question, I think that there's so much fear, courtesy of this propaganda, that even the thought of resistance brings thoughts of pain and suffering. I think we should have a strategy. I don't think we have a strategy for the most part.

So, you know, whether we should change it or not, I think we should develop one that's coherent and cohesive, that we can stick by. We talk about the referendum. The referendum was to vote to see if you can vote against Cop Cities. If we're going to have a referendum on the table, it needs to be about community control of public safety.

If we're going to have a referendum on the table, it should be about decentralization. It should be about decertifying police unions. Those are the only referendums that are going to make sense. A referendum to vote on if you can have something on the ballot, it sounds about as ridiculous as possible. So, of course, I mean, you're asking, you know, it's like someone asked me recently how to get a permit.

I've been organizing for 39 years. So, someone said to me: Well, how do you get a permit to protest such and such? I said, I've never gotten a permit. Why do I have to seek permission to protest? Seek permission to tell you that I don't like how you treating me, you know. Can you give me a permit so I can, you know, resist that? That is illogical. So, resistance has to be at the top of the list.

Liliana: Oh, this … this, hits hard. I grew up in the middle of a civil war. I was in Colombia when Pablo Escobar was hiding, and there were so many American soldiers just on the hunt, and they weren't using uniforms. They were you know, we kind of knew who they were because they were tall, white, blue eyes. So, it wasn't too hard to know who they were.

We have a bombing every night for months. I remember every time we hear the boom, the windows shaking. We didn't have cell phones at the time. It was like the early nineties. My mom would walk in the kitchen very slow. She'll grab the phone and she'll call all her kids just to make sure we were fine.

We were having so many massacres all over the country: twenty here, fifty here; everywhere. I moved to my sister's house because we lost our home. So, I had to move to my sister's house, and just in that one street, the kids that I played with, they were taken by the cops. Then they disappeared. We never saw them again. And that was in a two-year period, and we saw the media talking about the guerrillas, the guerrillas, how cruel there were, and they're making the country look bad. They're doing this and they're doing that. The whole country was experiencing a lot of violence. But in my particular case, I was lucky enough to be in a home in the city with family, But, most of the people in the mountains, the guerrillas, there were displaced, most of them witnessed their mothers being raped and killed by soldiers, many of them. Saw their little sisters had their head cut off right in front of their eyes. So, yes, a lot of the rebels, a lot of guerrillas did a lot of stuff that I'm sure they're not proud of, but what I say, I wish I was able to talk to these people in the media like it's so easy to criminalize and to judge when you are on the other side of the river. Colombia's been—if not number one— one of the countries that has so many graduates from the School of the Americas.

I think Colombia's been one of the, if not number one, one of the countries who gets more financial aid, military aid from the U.S. We're still, every single year, we're still number one when it comes to the number of organizers killed. We have at least 200 killed every single year, and that number is the number in the records.

But we know the number is way bigger than that. We have so many people missing, disappear every single day. These people never make it to the record. We don't know because since there's no body, they can't put these people as deaths. But we know that 200 is a very small number. We know. Every single year we had the most organizers killed every year. And we have environmentalists killed every year. We're always number one. And we're still number one producing cocaine. All this money that Colombia gets from the U.S. is going to pay death squads, police, military, and it's not doing anything against the cartels. No, it's making things worse and worse. To me resistance is a beautiful word, but we've been paying a big price for it.

I don't think resistance is a right. I think resistance is our duty and it's necessary, it's our duty by any means. Resistance.

James: I appreciate [the clarity], even though it's so painful. In the *Beyond Cop Cities* chapter "Combat Police Terror," authors Dhoruba bin Wahad and Kalonji Changa write about the decertification and recertification of police unions:

> to reform or rethink policing in America without a full appreciation and understanding of the actual danger militarized policing poses to legitimate democracy is impossible. Meaningful reform of policing cannot be achieved without an appreciation given that America is controlled by armed state agents posing as, quote, civil servants, end quote, who are controlled by corporate donors, but yet are funded by taxpayer dollars while remaining beyond public accountability. (p. 88)

Predatory systems make us dance in a death cycle by taking our money to pay for this structured violence. Veterans for Peace or different organizations over the decades have challenged and will continue to challenge it. When I hear Kalonji and Liliana, I feel that this is a call for our people to come home.

We understand everybody needs some kind of job to pay the bills, put food on the table, get health insurance for family and kids. But this loyalty or devotion or the belief that if you joined the army or police forces, that somehow you can be in a community that has decency, love, and honor rather than dishonor, that's a fantasy. We are all linked in different ways. My happiest years as a kid playing stickball, kickball was on the Ft. Benning, Georgia lands that held the School of the Americas (SOA). My father was a military officer for years. He might have worked at SOA. Our contradictions are embedded in family, our nonprofits, academia … there's a whole list that goes on and on.

We have to agree to the terms of reality. I agree with what's been put on the table: self-defense is not an act of violence. In seminary I met women who were going to start nonprofits against domestic violence; they were very clear after meetings that you have the right to self-defense if you're being battered in the household or on the street. That resistance is not an act of violence. That is an act of love. We would have to abide by that, a certain kind of spirit, despite the fear and the pain that we've been talking about. This is one of those occasions where we start talking about a book and end up revealing that we're talking about our lives, desires, fears— but also our commitments and courage.

The state doesn't win, because we're not predictable if we love deeply. Nobody's going to forecast the future or give you a play-by-play book for resistance. But we will do what is necessary—as Liliana said; and, because it is necessary, we have commitment.

Liliana: Last week, the head of the Southern Command, the general, Laura Richardson, went to Latin America and she was interviewed about the U.S. concerns about Latin America, blah, blah, blah. Her main concern was the influence of China and Putin in Latin America. She was afraid they were going after Latin America's resources. She talked about Venezuelan oil, the water, all the resources, saying "*our* water," "*our* oil." I guess she forgot that she was talking in public. She was referencing Latin American resources but she was talking about her belongings. I think that is how the School of the Americas, U.S. American Army bases [and forts function] throughout the world. It's like they own everything. That is how they feel [powerful through] entitlement. They [think they] own everything. And that is why we're doing this [intervention].

CHAPTER THREE

1492: Indigenous Sovereignty, Black Self-Determination amid Repression[1]

Mohamed Abdou, Ashanti Alston, interview by Kalonji Changa, Joy James

Kalonji Changa: Mohamed Abdou, you've been catching a lot of hell, and that's an understatement. You've had death threats, folks trying to "whitelist" you—what most call blacklisting. They've been coming at you pretty hard. We know that you've been on the scene over at Columbia University. Your tweets have been gangster. They've taken your tweets to Congress to talk about this terrible Mohamed Abdou and how he's just a menace to society, and he's pro-Palestinian and anti-Zionist, which, I don't see anything wrong with. For folks who are not following [the repression of free speech and anti-genocide organizing], give us a little bit of background as to why you would be targeted. There are a whole lot of professors and students being attacked around the country and around the globe right now. Within this state of tyranny and oppression, under this violent regime, why are you so special?

Mohamed Abdou: First, Salaam Alaikum and Shalom Aleichem to our Jewish siblings who might be listening. I usually start anything that I often say out in public with Moses' prayer in the Quran. And Moses' prayer is "Oh Creator, open thy breast, and make my affairs easy, and undo the knot in my tongue."*

There are many ways in which one can talk about how this all evolved. The reason that I'm being targeted is because I'm casting doubt on the American dream. I'm calling it out for what it is that Malcolm X [el hajj Malik es Shabazz] had referred to as "an American nightmare."

---

* The prayer was spoken in Arabic and has been translated.

I am calling attention to 1492 and what happened to Muslims and Jews in Andalusia and Spain, in terms of forced conversion, persecution, murder. The reference too, is savages and heathens. Savage being the racial sort of descriptor, and heathen being the religious. Obviously underneath the auspices of Ferdinand and Isabella, but also how that links to Columbus's invasion of the Americas, manifest destiny, doctrines of discovery, *terra nullius*. Indigenous people were referred to as savages and heathens. Hernán Cortés had referred to Aztec women as Moorish women, Aztec temples, all 400 of them, as Moorish mosques. He referred to Montezuma, the Aztec leader, as a Sultan. Even the term "berdache," that was used to describe Two Spirit Indigenous people, was first cast upon gender-nonconforming Muslims. And then, of course, with settler colonialism here, the very monster 531 years of ongoing genocide. That project continued after the murder of … millions of Indigenous people [see "How Colonization of the Americas Killed 90% of Their Indigenous People—and Changed the Climate", *YES!*, February 13, 2019] with transatlantic slavery, with the middle passage, "afterlife of slavery" projects as Saidiya Hartman had referred to it: stand-your-ground laws, school-to-prison pipelines.

Our Black siblings were Muslims from the Iberian Peninsula and the west coast of Africa. So, I'm talking about how America is a crusading project that continues on to this day. Of course, you know the white man having appropriated Christianity and Eastern tradition, weaponized it underneath Constantine as an imperial instrument of conquest. That's why I'm being outed, because I'm saying that we don't only have a genocide insofar as Palestine, but ultimately that the genocide continues here, and we need to contend with that.

The serpent snake, as Frederick Douglass referred to her, America. And here I'm calling out immigrants and immigrant settlers of color. Of course, Indigenous people are the caretakers of the land, and Black people, who are descendants of the Middle Passage, I don't consider them to be settlers. This is a discussion that we sensibly have to sit down and talk about, because there wasn't the element of choice. But here I'm referring to immigrant settlers of color. I'm talking about South Asians, North Africans, Arabs, Muslims and so on, that buy into the American dream, upward

CONFRONTING COUNTERINSURGENCY

ascendancy, mobility, "civilization," assimilation into the settler-colonial society. The structure that is, as Patrick Wolfe referred to, settler colonialism, is not an event, it set up a structure, and we need to understand that structure, because, as Kwame Ture noted, there is a difference between mobilization and organization. Organization is about understanding structures. And, perhaps this is something that we'll talk about. The fact is, we should be able to live in a world together, where with our faith or our lack of faith, and despite them, we can have dialogues across our differences. If not for ourselves or the sake of Mother Earth, for the sake of our children, who as Mumia Abu-Jamal has noted, "come from immortality and are the arrows that we shoot towards infinity."

Of course, that isn't being permitted. That isn't being allowed because the architects of animosity, be it Shafik Minouche, be it you know Congress woman Stefanik,* or Congress in general, be it "Genocide Joe," be it Trump, be it the mainstream media. Whether it's Fox News, liberal, conservative, CNN and so on—they amplify in hyperbolic ways the animosities or the differences that exist, just to create schisms between us. It's for these reasons that I became a target. It's because I'm casting doubt on the American dream, and not just calling out the genocide that Israel is certainly complicit in, that Zionists[2] are complicit in.

Joy James: There's this weird alliance of reactionaries. Shafik is Egyptian and the [former] president of Columbia University.† This whole integrationist project is an integration into empire. If I'm understanding you, this is a desire to belong to empire. It suggests that people would lie their tongues off in order to be embedded in an imperial project. What you, the students, and the professors who

---

* Minouche is the former President of Columbia University; Elise Stefanik, NY-Republican, according to *The New York Times* and *NBC*, supported the "great replacement" rhetoric of white nationalism throughout her political career. Overlooked in April 2025 to be an ambassador in the Trump administration, she remains in the House of Representatives.
† Shafik resigned in August 2024 and as at spring 2025 Columbia has had several interim presidents.

support them, as well as other activists and organizers [are doing] is very brave and courageous. It is also deeply spiritual.

From 1492, when Arabs and Africans were defeated in Spain and the so-called Moors pushed out, to [the funding of Christopher Columbus to invade and conquer the Indigenous in the Americas] to the present day, we've been [forced into] this barbaric dance by the piper, which is capital and imperialism. So many people who look like us have agreed to go along with the tune.

Abdou: The key is that whiteness isn't just a color of skin. It is also that. It's a phenotype. It's a privilege. I mean, hell, people of color, we've been tamed. We've been weaned to resent our own color of skin. We will bleach our skin white. This is the degree of internal resentment that we've cultivated. Shame. What Frantz Fanon had referred to as the "inferiority complex" in *Black Skin, White Masks*. What I prefer to focus on is that it's nobody's fault that they're born white, and there are Arabs that are white passing. Whiteness is a certain power; it's a certain complicity. It's a certain privilege because of the structures that it's embodied within. This is why I prefer to focus on cultures of whiteness, which even BIPOC people have internalized. And what are acronyms? We have Black Indigenous people, Black people of color, LGBTQ, but that's the governing order that the white man had handed over for us to conceptualize, perceive of ourselves, and to make ourselves perceptible to one another, even as people of color.

People of color have internalized cultures of whiteness. This becomes part of the problem. You know, at this white phenomenon called the Black Skin, White Masks, right? Brown Skin, White Masks. And, we can talk about Red Skin, White Masks.[3] Minouche Shafik is sort of an embodiment of that assimilationist project, precisely as you noted. 1492 becomes very important because of the spiritual arc, because of the presumption of secularism that masks its Christian ethos. White Christian ethos. Again, Protestant conceptualizations of property that this nation is founded upon, Victorian notions of gender and sexuality, manifest destiny, doctrines of discovery, *terra nullius*.

43

The left has become so antagonistic to this question of spirituality. And of course, we'd have to talk about the difference between spirituality and faith and religion, because these are three interrelated concepts, but they're not one and the same thing. We'd have to talk about authoritarian and non-authoritarian and non-institutionalized conceptualizations of religion. So, this is what becomes key. It figures into the equation that way, and the way that leftists embody this anti-spiritual aspect. Well, we'd have to rethink that, because, as Kwame Ture had noted, you can't be revolutionary without being religious.[4] Then we have the examples of Nat Turner, we have the examples of Malcolm X [el-Hajj Malik el-Shabazz], of MLK [Rev. Martin Luther King, Jr.] and so many others. The embodiment of a political, theological, social justice project that, in my humble opinion, is founded in all faiths. Where is Jesus that stood beside Mary Magdalene, that flipped the table on the money exchangers in the temples, where's Muhammad who stood for the oppressed? Where's Moses who stood before and fought against Pharaoh? This becomes the question. And there is no puritanism here. Look, Myanmar and the government there has constructed the militarized, conservative interpretation of Buddhism to use against the Rohingya. Islamophobia is this linchpin that everybody uses, from China against the Uyghurs, and certainly in the case of Hindutva against Dalits, Kashmiris and so on? And Malayali people who are Christian are lumped underneath that umbrella.

It's not that Islam is exceptional to me, but it has become constructed as the quintessential other, given the history of 1492. What Islam has come to figure in the mind of the white Crusader, especially when we're talking about Indigenous land defenders and water protectors being referred to as Jihadi terrorists by paramilitary organizations which are extensions of the military industrial complex. Even Black Lives Matter protesters are being labeled as Black extremist groups. This becomes the figuration of Islam, and one can't really contend with race or understand it without understanding spirituality and religion, and the way they intersect historically and the way that both impact one another in terms of racial projects, but also the religious animus that informs that component. That becomes the key.

I'm trying to also transcend neoconservative interpretations of this Islam. Because what I'm saying is that, hey, I'm with and for anti-colonial resistance. I'm with the arc of resistance. However, I got issues with the resistance. I got issues with Hamas. I got issues with Hezbollah. I got issues with any movement or any state, for that matter, that embodies authoritarianism, that embodies sexist, racist, misogynist, queerphobic sort of tendencies. And that isn't just exclusive to Hamas or Hezbollah. These ills exist on the left, that embodies queerphobia, that embodies anti-blackness, and a lot of other things. And they exist, of course, on the right. That's the idea behind *Islam and Anarchism* and using the Quran, because whether you're a part of the Nation of Islam, whether you're Sunni, whether Shiite—I don't identify with any of these sects, ultimately, you're beholden to the Quran. It becomes the barometer by which I'm able to gauge. The beauty about Malcolm is that he always engaged in these projects of metamorphosis. The Malcolm before and after the Nation of Islam is not the same as the Malcolm before and after Mecca. What would Malcolm say about his friendship with regards to a queer Black man, James Baldwin? How would that have led him, insofar as his understanding of queerness?

In my mind, I'm not going to have to choose between the false binary of a Zionist crusading Wahhabi project on the one hand, and a Russian, Chinese totalitarian project on the other hand. Those are false choices. There are alternative forms of governance beyond the white man's nation state, the master's tools will never dismantle the master's house, as Audre Lorde had taught us. We see capitalism as a product of colonial modernity. But what about the nation state? This is what white supremacists were supporting just a few years ago. "Jews will not replace us" kind of narratives in Charleston. This is the façade of it all: all of a sudden, they care about Jewish people. Trump and the alt right and so on.

James: Baldwin loved Malcolm. I so appreciate your work, because there's a fluidity. There's always a lot in the flow. Baldwin becomes a survivor of these siblings. Everybody knows Baldwin is queer, and they also know he's brilliant. They also know Baldwin [could no longer tolerate living] in this country. Baldwin is going to be an expat [but still loves America] as was Nina Simone: "I'm in France, I would rather not be in the American project, but I'm going to write and critique it." Medgar Evers was assassinated in 1963, Malcolm in 1965 (his daughters are working with Ben Crump to sue the NYPD, FBI, CIA, for the state's alleged roles in that assassination). Then King is assassinated in 1968. Artist Sam Cook [who organized and associated with Malcolm, Baldwin, etc.] also dies violently [at the hands of a Black woman who is not prosecuted]. These men all loved each other, even if isolated, banned because of his politics would be Malcolm; banned because of their sexuality would be Baldwin. Raoul Peck's documentary *I Am Not Your Negro* does not mention that Baldwin is queer. So, my question to you: How could we more clearly see our vulnerability, but also our strength and resistance if we agreed not to engage in what Felicia Denaud described as "Western fundamentalism"? There is a reactionary, proto-fascist religiosity in the United States, which has been secularized. Conservatives sprinkle stardust from billionaires on top of that fundamentalism, and pretend it is not incredibly poisonous. So how is it that our relationship with liberalism, with the desire to belong, with the desire to be safe, can be disrupted and stabilized by spirituality at the same time?

Abdou: Joy, contending with your question means that we need to transition from talking about resistance to talking about liberation. Resistance, to me, is reactionary. Liberation is active. We keep on talking about surviving, but what about thriving? This is an active stance. Going back to Fanon, when the colonized other sees an image of themselves, or as we have been exposed to colonialism over the course of 531 years, we develop these reactionary stances. Part of it is a religious component in terms of how we tend to see our relationship to spirituality.

One can look at Algeria, for instance, with the FLN [National Liberation Front], women were very much a part of the resistance against the French. They weren't necessarily hijabs or anything like that. And once you overthrow your colonizer, because you want to distance yourself from anything remotely associated with whiteness, and because you're just acting in reactionary self-defense formations, you're not even allowed the ability to reconfigure your own traditions, to understand what the colonizer had done in relationship to you, in relationship to land. The question also goes back to land. Land configures everything, not only our spirituality, because she is a spiritual subject, right? She's not an object. But it configures time, space, gender relations, the private, the public. To take a step back and to be able to rethink about what happened in the case of Algeria is the fact that a lot of men turned to conservative interpretations of Islam and said, "Okay, well, we want to distance from anything remotely white. And you women, you go back home, you wear your hijabs." And in a certain sense, that is part of the formulation that led to the "Civil War." I don't consider it to be much of a civil war. I don't think there are many civil wars, as much as they are proxy wars.

We can look at it in examples such as Daesh, ISIS, which is a reactionary movement, albeit extreme, supported by the West, and certainly Zionists and Saudi Arabia and Wahhabisms. We're talking about 14-year-olds, 15-year-olds that left their homes in the UK. They've never lived in Iraq or in Syria, but ISIS had broken those arbitrary dividing, colonizing boundaries between Iraq and Syria. That arbitrary border that colonialism had drawn. And these 14- and 15-year-olds went and they wanted to be a part of the Ummah, or the conceptualization of the Ummah, which is the community of Muslims and believers generally, together, alike, at least that's its traditional understanding. But in this case, they vied for a conservative interpretation of Islam because they thought that this is the way to assert their dignity, their sense of self, self-respect, in puritan living, but in purely reactionary formations.

I am speaking from the position of privilege. The opportunity to decolonize this, sit down and engage in abolitionist understandings of Islam, to get to know ourselves and our traditions. Again, I mean, obviously there's no going back to the time of the Prophet or Moses or Jesus or 1492, but what we want to extract are the ethical, political, spiritual commitments and begin to deploy them in the present. If I understand your question correctly, it requires our taking a pause and actually rethinking. This is why Fanon said decolonization is inherently a violent act. Violent not at the level of just tactics or defense or self-defense, but at the level of the crisis of the self, the double consciousness that Du Bois had spoken about. Figuring ourselves out, not only in relationship to who we are, we in relationship to Islam, in relationship to other people, given Arab supremacy, given anti-blackness. I'm an Egyptian. I was born in Egypt. Well, Egypt, you know, thrives on its construction. Arabs now thrive, particularly in the context of Egypt, on disavowing their Nubian lineages and descent and constructing ourselves as the whites of the Middle East. Of course, there's the elements of queerphobia and so on, because of the disruption of our relationship to land as people of color, and masculinities and femininities that are tied to the private and the public.

Changa: With all these assaults that are happening, given this condition of war that we've been born into, it is very challenging, because the inclination is to simply say, "Well, I'm an immigrant here. I just want to be a part of the dream. I just want to live. I just want to survive. I just want to make ends meet." That is where community becomes important. This is where the experience of the Panthers is important as Ashanti, you know, insofar as organization [is concerned], we're even far away from that. The potential of these Palestine solidarity encampments offered a different world, where different people, different formations, may walk with one another, not *on* one another. May walk with the land and allow the land to teach them something, because she's a spiritual subject that has much to answer or much to teach us, beyond historical material analysis that doesn't account for metaphysics. I mean, this is the lab that produces the air that we breathe, the seeds that blossom into fruits and vegetables.

I shudder to think that Muslims, we sit down and read the Quran. So many chapters in the Quran are named after non-human life— the chapter of the bees, the chapter of the sun, the chapter of the moon, the chapter of the thunder—but we don't sit down and reflect on the wisdom of Allah Subhanahu Wa Ta'ala in teaching us all this. It also requires that we think and go beyond identity politics. As I always say, it doesn't matter to me if somebody comes and introduces themselves as a Muslim or if they're queer, they're Black, or they're

Indigenous. You could be Muslim and Zionist. There are plenty of those nowadays. So, what are the ethical, political, spiritual commitments that inform one's identities? That's what the coming formations and communities need to contend with. America is leading this war-crusading. America is leading this war without the assertion of Indigenous sovereignty and Black self-determination, and particularly Indigenous sovereignty, that tends to be neglected because of how U.S. history constructs itself from 1619 onwards. The original sin is masked, and Indigenous people are regarded as like signposts to history, unless their names are on football teams like the Washington Redskins or the Chiefs, or their names are on weapons of mass destruction like Tomahawk missiles and Apache helicopters.

James: At a [December 20, 2022] conference at Yale [titled "Incarceration and Imagination"], one panelist insisted that "We don't need prayer." I [understood that they saw prison Christianity and ministers as oppressive]. However, I responded that militants also align with religion ... there are Muslim names among the revolutionaries, like Assata Shakur, [Dhoruba Bin-Wahad, Safiyah Bukhari, Ashanti Alston, Jihad Abdulmumit, Sekou Odinga]. So, the notion of prayer has been "Christianized" in the U.S., even if the persons are Jewish [Buddhist, Muslim].

A Brown University workshop discussed the murder of George Floyd, and why didn't somebody "throw a cell phone." We capture the torture, digitize and narrate torture and the death. But are [we] rebelling? What spiritual stability can we learn from the Panthers and people who went underground, understanding that there are contradictions.... People went to prison for all those years based on principle and "revolutionary love." How is it that those of us who cannot or will not engage on that level of resistance can comprehend [this form of love for community or hatred for repression]?

At academic talks, people sometimes mock spirituality. The people who went underground—the hypocenter—differ from those who stayed at the epicenter, the surface of politics.[5] I see the spirituality in the people who take the risks. Mohamed, you took risks too, as did the students at Columbia, and Brown, all the students who were arrested, brutalized by the police [and assailants]. Students got jacked up at UCLA [USC, and UC-Irvine], by cops, but also by white nationalists. [Administrations and police allowed aggressors to] roll up on campus and inflict harm on people protesting genocide; most of the assailants were not arrested for their brutality.... If our revolutionaries carry spirit, we all do to some degree. How is it that we recognize what they carry when we are afraid or cannot do what they do?

Changa: One of the grand arguments on this platform [is about] the necessity of spirituality when it comes to revolution. Maybe I'm not as revolutionary as a lot of people, but for me, it's the mental, physical, and the spiritual. It's the spiritual side that has motivated so many of our freedom fighters. So many of the freedom fighters that I know are primarily Muslim or they come out of Ifa or Indigenous African spirituality. I hear folks all the time saying, they mock spirituality. We understand your disdain for religion. But when it comes to spirituality, it's like saying that I don't need my brain to think, I don't need my mind.

Ashanti Alston: Some of that is generational. I got some comrades from back in the old days. We go at it sometimes, and are stuck in stuff that was so scientific. It wasn't big as science, Marxism, Leninism, and all the other isms, if it wasn't that guiding it, it didn't have much to do with other things. Forgetting the fact that we are humans, we are much bigger than the sciences. That you have to deal with human beings on a very multi-dimensional level. Anyone who asks "What do we need to be praying about?" in so many words [needs to come] to an understanding that we, not only just being an *African* people, we're a spiritual people, just as people. You can't just deal with us as just people. You can't just deal with a class analysis. And I think that's one of the things that I really appreciate about Mohamed's book, because it brings in more of a holistic perspective.

Abdou: Marxism, has Marxism not become a religion? Anarchism, not a religion? Capitalism has its own religion. The state has its own religion: "In God We Trust" on the dollar bill, promises to protect against all enemies, foreign and domestic. You're pledging allegiance to a sovereign, and you can't pledge allegiance to two sovereigns simultaneously at the same time.

I was listening to these conservatives recently talking about how Americans should just be Americans, in the sense that they shouldn't hold dual passports or citizenships, because that puts them at odds in so far as their pledges of allegiance. So, what are we pledging allegiance to? You could call it God, Yahweh, Mother Earth, Buddha. It doesn't matter. It's irrelevant to them. But the covenant that one holds with a sovereign, that becomes the question.

I understand the impulse. Human beings like to control, right? We want to see it, to define it. But that's part of the European gaze, the white man's gaze, that unless it is categorizable, subject to discipline, subject to something that we control, then it must not hold true. Even from the perspective of those on the other end. I mean, the United Arab Emirates and the Arabian Gulf peninsula countries are actually conscripting Muslim scholars in the West, in order to make the argument for the legitimacy of the Abraham Accords.[6] So regardless of even if you don't believe in God, that's okay, fine, right? This is why I said it's the faith or the lack of faith. But that becomes part of the revolutionary equation because it's part of the propaganda tools that the other side is using, like it or not. So how are you responding to that?

Let me frame it another way, how can one love without spirit? Because it also assumes this calculus, right? Or dialectical materialism, historical materialism, right? It assumes the surgical narrative, where it's one, two, three, and our species has got it all figured out. We have crowned ourselves as Gods, and revolution is just a series of steps that we need to participate in. Again, what about the cosmos, what about our Earth, that ultimately is above everything else. Our Mother Earth doesn't need us. We need her. We're at the bottom of the pyramid, as opposed to, again, our construction of ourselves at the very top. But this assumption that we don't need metaphysics, that we don't need cosmology, it's part of our arrogance that we assume that we have nothing to learn from the universe, and the calculability of it all. Well, if that's the case, then why haven't we institutionalized or instituted some kind of change? Where is the sense of modesty, of humility that becomes necessary, in my humble opinion, for a revolutionary? In fact, it's one of the most defining important characteristics, and a sense of accountability to a higher principle, a higher sense of community, a higher level of justice and judgment, adjudication.

People are talking about mass conversion, reversion rates that are happening in the U.S. It's sort of like a post-9/11 moment. My concern is, what Islam are you converting or reverting to? Is it a conservative Islam or a liberal Islam, or what kind of Islam? I mean, that becomes more important, because it's not a matter of numbers. As the Prophet, peace be upon him, had said, "near the end of times, Muslims will be as many as the foam of the oceans of the wave, but they will be fickle and feeble as that, as that wave when it crashes into the rocks." It's not a matter of numbers. The Panthers weren't large in numbers. The Zapatistas aren't large in numbers. The Quran says, "How many of a small group defeated the larger enemy?" But that becomes the element of conviction, that needs to be embodied. So, to go back to not only the question of spirituality, how do we organize in such a way to establish a certain stability? And I think it's going to be the shift, again, from mobilization to organization. We have these direct actions, these mass mobilizations, which are far less than the anti-war protests that never stopped the Iraq War.

Again, it's not a matter of numbers. We have conservative Muslims that are against critical race theory and feminism and queerness, and right next to them, we got queers of all strands and stripes, and anti-Zionist Jews, and right next to them, an Islamophobic and anti-spiritual left. And everybody's yelling, "Free, free, Palestine." And they're all projecting their ideological specters onto what a free Palestine is supposed to be, without talking about the differences between them, because there is no left, and the left eats each other apart. Marxist versus anarchist versus, I don't know who, and so on and so forth. There is no ethics of disagreement or conflict resolution mechanism. Or an ethics of hospitality by which we get to know one another, because that's where trust is built. We're able to again engage in that. What is an inherent violence to the self is us getting to know one another, again, vis-à-vis the stereotypes that we've internalized of one another. There isn't organization at that

52

level. We aren't breaking bread. We aren't looking each other eye to eye. We aren't building with one another, and we aren't establishing a sense of community. I think that is an inherently spiritual act, religion or not, because it involves an investment in another's spirits, in another's cosmology, worldview, and being open to the fact that one will be altered, one will change.

The process of meeting somebody is also a process. I mean, it's a beautiful moment knowing somebody's name that is to be offered and not to be solicited or interrogated that way. But it's a spiritual moment, because anything can attract or repel two people, a scent, a look, a gesture, a word, unintended. And I always believe that there's an outside spirit that brings two souls together, right, and binds them together. And out of an appreciation of that, it also becomes a moment of mourning that at some point I or the other is going to die, there isn't a human being that has been created on this Earth that has not passed away at some point or another, but it's then recognizing the feebleness, the fragility, the finiteness of life that is endowed with a certain spirited camaraderie, kinship, and that's what demands the kind of investment. So yeah, to me, that's the question of spirituality.

Changa: As you talk about spirituality, you speak on community. There is Columbia University, and over 50 other university encampments in the United States, and also dozens around the world. It seems like some form of community, even if it's not the community that we envision. You've been one of many professors who has been attacked. President Shafik took parts of your tweets, she and Congresswoman Stefanik had this conversation that made you look like some pro-Hamas lunatic [seeking] to burn it all down. Why do you think Shafik willingly lied when she said that you were no longer employed at Columbia University, and that you would never be hired again at the university? In the streets, Zionists were calling you all types of names and [making] death threats. The spiritual part is necessary. Let's talk about what's going on physically right now.

Abdou: Thank you for your questions. Now, there are two parts to this. Again, going back to the question of, why am I being targeted?

It wasn't the fact that she was just blacklisting me universally in terms of a job that I am an expert in and I was hired for. I was hired to be an interdisciplinary scholar. I was teaching a course on queer and feminist BIPOC traditions from abolitionist and decolonial perspectives. But I was hired also because of my organizing background with the Zapatistas, the post-Seattle anti-globalization movements, the anti-war protests, to expose the students to actual social movement organizing, and what that means from a social movement lens. Theory is a revolutionary praxis, as the late bell hooks says. So those were the skill sets that brought me here, from the land grab, Zionist Cornell University.

It is that, and the fact that faculty and students were actively lobbying to have me stay after my tenure. My contract ends on May 30, 2024. She lied, as you noted, with regard to my being terminated. But to lobby to have me stay in another position, given the fact that, hey, I can teach in gender studies, Middle Eastern, African and South Asian Studies. My work deals with Indigenous Studies, with Black Studies. I work on Political Theology. Over 50 students had signed a petition, a letter that they wrote and had taken the initiative to write to the chair of the department, asking for the course to be offered next year. These were active efforts. [The administration] didn't like the fact that I was very much involved with the students organizing on the ground, or at least mobilizing at the time. The right picked up on that. They picked up on the fact that I was at the encampments. I was the first professor, and I think the only professor, that actually actively taught inside the encampment. They were losing their minds, "Is he terminated or not? We're seeing him at the encampment." Of course, I've been photographed unbeknownst to me, walking into the building or my office building, let alone to the encampments. I was never terminated. My entry onto campus was never revoked. But I've also had folks, like conservatives, like David Rubin, put out videos on YouTube and they're picking up on the imminent threats that I ostensibly pose, calling out the American dream, because David Rubin comes about and says, "Oh, he's arguing for Indigenous rights." Actually, I'm arguing for Indigenous sovereignty. And he goes out and says something lunatic: "I guess that Mohamed Abdou would be okay with a Native

American walking inside his building and blowing it up." It's quite surreal that his video is available online. He's got 2.4 million followers. My point being that him, others, Stefanik attacking me online, but also others going through my "CUNY for Palestine" event, "Oh, he speaks in spoken word poetry. Oh, he's talking about black self-determination." They're clearly understanding, although they're misconstruing, that what I'm after is not only a project of resistance, but a project of liberation.

Hamas and Hezbollah are not liberatory to me, not a project that is anchored in general liberation, and they fail to understand that liberation as decolonization as abolition, is not about destruction. It's about creation of a purest first world, a world of many worlds, a world of the below, for the poor, for the dispossessed, for the elderly, for children, for queer and gender dissidents. An anti-authoritarian world, a non-authoritarian world, a non-capitalist world. You know revolutions of all practical questions, the transformation of ourselves, the greater jihad, the combat against our inner micro-fascisms. Because to put it into plain words, what are you going to do when you get sick? These are the questions. What are you going to do with the army, with the police. What are you going to do when you know somebody gets hungry? This is why revolutions evolve. What are you creating in terms of an alternative? And that's what the left lacks. It doesn't create alternatives in so many ways. It wants to dismantle whatever exists, which is an investment in the settler-colonial order. But what if we divest from it? The Panthers created the breakfast programs. They took over their own neighborhoods, and started organizing. The Zapatistas, they emerged on the scene ten years after they had been preparing alternative schools, ways of conceiving of healing, of food sovereignty and so on.

So as to the death threats, yeah, people recognize me on the street. I was just walking with my friend Maura Finkelstein this morning, meeting for the first time, and somebody that was sitting down outside on a patio just yelled out, "Dr Abdou, you suck!" But that's the least of it. I mean, I'm getting emails that are saying "You're lucky, dude, that you're standing upright. We know who you are. We know where you are." Bring it back to the encampments and the possibilities, because these students, they allowed us to dream dangerously, right? I think that these youth allow that, and that's their inspiration, the way they created safe spaces. And safe spaces that had conditions and rules: no drugs, no alcohol, no sexual harassment. At the public library, they had a clinic, a medic center. Prayer was a part of it. Community was a part of it. Festivity was a part of it. They learned how to mourn death, how to celebrate life. What they were against, what these encampments are against, be it UCLA or otherwise, just so that it's very clear, I think it's clear to us, they aren't just combating a Board of Trustees, they aren't just combating Columbia University that's a badly managed real estate corporation with investments and, you know, Amazon, Heiko, Lockheed Martin, dual degree programs in Tel Aviv. They're doing something more than that. They're against the settler state, and this is beyond the new McCarthyism, because Islamophobia is at the heart of local, as well as foreign policy. Students have been exposed to microwave hearing LRAD [long-range acoustic device] weapons that are used to suppress dissent. They've been exposed to eviction; they're exposed to jail. They've been exposed to suspension, and they had to be suspended in order for the police to come into campus. Police were called twice. What they did at Hinds Hall had happened on four separate, different occasions, taking over what was referred to as Hamilton Hall.

To break it down, back to Cop City. We had NYC Mayor Eric Adams—this Pinocchio, the second to Donald Trump in his wanton mendacity, and who wants to retire in Israel—being called in, and the NYPD arrests over 300 students, close to 2,500 nationally. Eric Adams claimed that the students were radicalized. And of course, there's nothing illegal about being radicalized. This is the irony, right? He wants to suppress First Amendment rights. But okay, let's put that aside. He refers to the students as being influenced by professional outside agitators, which is a racist discourse, as we know. It's a racist term that emerges out of the Jim Crow era and Civil Rights Movement activists and someone being labeled as such. We have NYPD Chief of Patrol, John Chell, who was central in the planning of the execution of both raids at Columbia, who actually murdered Ortanzso Bovell in 2008. He shot him in the back, and now mistakenly, he fired his gun while they were retaking Hinds Hall, like a student could have been killed. One of our kids could have been killed. And they do it all the time. And the madness about this moment, if I may say, is that it's going in and out. Right, the global, the local. It's just like not too long ago, we're at the Arab Spring. Then we moved to Occupy. Occupy what exactly? We're talking about stolen land. Then we were at No Dakota Pipeline. Then we were talking about the Black Spring, as Robin D.G. Kelley calls it. And now we've moved on to Palestine, and there's a genocide in the Congo when we're scrolling through genocide on phones mined from another genocide of copper and cobalt in the Congo. And what, there are no Trayvon Martins, Michael Browns, George Floyds, Breonna Taylors happening right now? I mean, what links these struggles together becomes the importance of a narrative that binds our struggles together, from a spiritual, from a political, from an ethical perspective.

Let's go back to this, the circus, and I'm sorry to call it that, in which, again, a student could have been killed. We have hilarious top NYPD Deputy Commissioner Daughtry holding a book titled *An Introduction to Terrorism Online*. The NYPD is releasing these videos, sophisticated videos, to prove how successful the raid was, and they show that they've found an introduction to terrorism, a book written by renowned historian Charles Townsend, and calling it a guide to terrorism. We had them showing bike chains on national television that students had used, bike chains that you could just buy from a store on campus. And again, Hamilton Hall was a significant site because it's been a site of student protests in '68 and '72 during the anti-war, anti-Vietnam War protests, in '85, protests against South African apartheid and calls for divestments. In 1996, students pulled off a hunger strike demanding that there be a department of ethnic studies.

So, it isn't a new thing, but here we have again kids being exposed to tear gas, flash bombs, batons, and this crackdown that is also led and facilitated by Rebecca Weiner. Weiner is a Columbia professor who leads the NYPD terrorism unit division that maintains an office at Tel Aviv. She [labels] student rhetoric [for a ceasefire] as terroristic. We had the NYPD literally on campus, and it's not like BIPOC people are safe with them on campus. We all know that.

But also accounts of them engaging in sexual assault, while faculty were forbidden from campus up until a few days ago. Students were forbidden from campus, I think they're actually forbidden from campus till today, because today is the last day in which the NYPD is required to be on campus. The messaging is one and the same. The *Washington Post* wrote an article yesterday divulging, and this is the confluence again of racial capitalism, of settler security states, that there were actually WhatsApp chat groups among some of the nation's most prominent billionaires and financial leaders with Adams. They included CEO of Starbucks, Howard Schultz, Dell founder and CEO Michael Dell, hedge fund manager, Bill Ackman and Joshua Kushner, the founder of Thrive capital and brother of Jared Kushner, Donald Trump's son-in-law, actually having chats with Adams about how these protests need to be ended.

James: The state is militarizing itself to protect capital. Around Cop Cities, billionaires are funding, in various ways, a private army. Eric Adams, you may vote for him because he's African American and you think that's a good look, but the function is what we care about.* It's not the identity, and that sort of brings me back to the whole captive maternal thing. It's really about the function. Columbia University hired an adjunct professor who does "counter terrorism" for the NYPD and also trains with the IDF and then designates the students as "proto terrorists" or terrorists in the making. That is their propaganda machine.

The security apparatus for protesters is imperative. We [can] build that in terms of concentric circles. When I went to Atlanta to meet people who had been in the forest, and knew Tortuguita, I asked them about their security apparatus. One young person could not articulate a security plan. Not because it wasn't supposed to be known to the public. It was because the security apparatus was not in place. When we talk about the Panthers, not in romantic or iconic terms, but focus on the function they had of feeding people, educating, etc., but they also provided security. That's why the original title

---

* See Alex N. Press, "Ten of Eric Adams's Worst Policies, Scandals, and Lies," *Jacobin*, April 17, 2024.

for the organization was the Black Panther Party *for Self-Defense*. We have the right to defend ourselves as Malcolm stated "by any means necessary." This is how you get Mabel and Robert Williams [authors of *Negroes with Guns*], the couple that headed a North Carolina NAACP but had to flee the country because the FBI persecuted them. They fled to Cuba, and ended up in China. Robert Williams asked Mao to write a statement that Black people have the right to self-defense; and he did.

We all have a right to self-defense. We're paying our tax money for the salaries and the pensions of the people who are harming us because we want to stop a genocide and stop billionaire ballers from determining the outcomes of social and economic life. Mohamed, you've been under incredible pressure, psychological, emotional, and it's a form of terrorism. The gender thing is weird given the celebrations for feminism but lack of critiques of the women presidents who are "liberals" yet aligned with repression. The students are trying to live up to UN protocols: Don't do war crimes.

If we balance the spirit with the security, we increase our capacity in deterring or pushing back predators. [Black] mayors can be predators, just like NYPD. They're not rogue. They've been talking to billionaires [who seek to run the city and the nation]. Mohamed and I work in this industry that makes platitudes about enlightenment and teaching students and caring about the world. Mohamed was teaching students in the encampment. When you actually have the care, love and decency to be an educator who is not an opportunist or a coward, that's when the [administration and state and police] try to delete or disappear you. Our role is to resist.

We talked a lot about Columbia where Mohamed taught. Remember the CUNY students [whose teeth were broken by police; they were given serious charges for largely peaceful protesting], and the arrests at the New School, as well as across the country. It's not just the elite or private schools [where students/faculty/staff are being battered and arrested, and fired or expelled from the university]. Profs have been fired, students pushed out, threatened, and doxed and blasted by reactionary press and police. So, thank you for your service, Mohamed.

PART II

BATTLING COLONIALISM

CHAPTER FOUR

Presentation to United Nations Special Committee on Decolonization: Committee Hearings on the Case of Puerto Rico

Benjamin Ramos Rosado

The ProLibertad Freedom Campaign
Thursday, June 23rd, 2024

Honorable members of the UN Special Committee on Decolonization, thank you, for this opportunity to be heard before this committee today.

The U.S. invaded Puerto Rico on July 25th, 1898.[1] The forced sterilization of Puerto Rican Women;[2] the 60-year bombing and poisoning of the island municipality of Vieques; the assassinations of Don Pedro Albizu Campos, Angel Rodriguez Cristobal, and Filiberto Ojeda Rios; the Ponce Massacre; the use of COINTELPRO against the Puerto Rican independence movement; and the incarcerations of the FALN* and *Los Macheteros* in the 1980s. This list is but a small sampling of the international human rights violations that the U.S. government has committed against the Puerto Rican nation in the 126 years since the U.S. invaded our island. If

---

* Fuerzas Armadas de Liberación Nacional (Armed Forces of National Liberation).

I were to recite the entire list of atrocities, it would take me another 126 years to finish.

Puerto Rico is a colony. This is an irrefutable fact. It is recognized by numerous international human rights organizations, academics, artists, activists, religious figures, and world leaders.

Since our colonization, we have been victims of U.S. economic and political exploitation and manipulation. There have been innumerable campaigns to eliminate our language, national identity, and culture. And, when we have revolted against these injustices, we were labeled "terrorists" and have either been assassinated or incarcerated. This repression is historically typical of a colonial relationship.

As a colonized people, we are victims of racism, xenophobia, and exploitation. The U.S. government has sponsored innumerable campaigns to wipe out our language, national identity, and culture. This type of genocide is in direct violation of international human rights laws and charters.

As I read this statement, the Puerto Rican nation is still suffering under the Colonial Fiscal Control Board. Installed by President Obama, this board has caused the closure of hospitals and schools, the elimination of pensions and retirement funds, and has caused rampant unemployment throughout the island. It pushed the passage of the LUMA Energy Contract, which has cost millions of dollars in lost revenue, furthered the dependency on fossil fuels, and increased the price of other basic services.

A Fiscal Control Board that has forced mass migration out of Puerto Rico. Forced relocation and economic refugee-ism are also historically typical of a colonial relationship.

Currently, the colonial government and the Fiscal Control Board have been championing Act 60, which was passed in 2019 and has created tax incentives for rich Americans and Europeans to gentrify the island. It has inspired and supported a wave of cryptocurrency colonizers like Brock Pierce and Social Media Moguls like Logan Paul to come to Puerto Rico to buy as much territory and homes as possible to fund their tourist ventures. Ventures which rarely employ Puerto Ricans and over-saturate their pockets because they barely pay taxes. All the while, Puerto Rican citizens are overtaxed and can barely survive. U.S. colonialism has made Puerto Rico a home for the rich who want to become richer.

There is a bill in Congress called, "The Puerto Rico Status Act" which pretends to resolve colonialism. The fact that this bill gives the U.S. government the power to approve or disapprove of our decolonization shows that the U.S. government has no desire to change their colonial control of Puerto Rico. The fact that State-hood is an option for decolonization is ridiculous and contradictory. The idea that the U.S. government is entitled to control and approve the mechanisms of our self-determination is dangerous. We support a decolonization process laid out by international law.

Honorable members, I ask this committee to stand with us, as you have before, and pass a resolution calling for an end to U.S. colonialism in Puerto Rico. We recommend that the case of Puerto Rico be brought to the United Nations General Assembly for review.

¡Que Viva Puerto Rico Libre! Free Puerto Rico!

CHAPTER FIVE

Oxford Union Address, Oxford University, November 28, 2024: Genocide: Israel and Palestine

susan abulhawa

Addressing the challenge of what to do about the Indigenous inhabitants of the land, Chaim Weizman, a Russian Jew, said to the World Zionist Congress in 1921 that Palestinians were akin to "the rocks of Judea, obstacles that had to be cleared on a difficult path." David Gruen, a Polish Jew, who changed his name to David Ben Gurion to sound relevant to the region, said. "We must expel Arabs and take their places." There are thousands of such conversations among the early Zionists who plotted and implemented the violent colonization of Palestine and the annihilation of her native people.

But they were only partially successful, murdering or ethnically cleansing 80% of Palestinians. This meant that 20% of us remained, an enduring obstacle to their colonial fantasies, which became the subject of their obsessions in the decades that followed, especially after conquering what remained of Palestine in 1967.

Zionists lamented our presence and they debated publicly in all circles—political, academic, social, and cultural—what to do with us; what to do about the Palestinian birthrate, about our babies, which they dub a "demographic threat." Benny Morris, who was originally meant to be here, once expressed regret that Ben Gurion "did not finish the job" of getting rid of us all, which would have obviated what they refer to as the "Arab problem."

Benjamin Netanyahu, a Polish Jew whose real name is Benjamin Mileikowsky, once bemoaned a missed opportunity during the 1989 Tiananmen Square uprising to expel large swaths of the Palestinian population "while world attention was focused on China."

Some of their articulated solutions to the nuisance of our existence include a "break their bones" policy in the '80s and '90s, ordered by Yitzhak Rubitzov, a Ukrainian Jew who changed his name to Yitzhak Rabin (for the same reasons).

That horrific policy crippling generations of Palestinians did not succeed in making us leave. And, frustrated by Palestinian resilience, a new discourse arose, especially after a massive natural gas field was discovered off the coast of Northern Gaza, worth trillions of dollars.

This new discourse is echoed in the words of Colonel Efraim Eitan, who said in 2004, "we have to kill them all."

Aaron Sofer, an Israeli so-called intellectual and political advisor, insisted in 2018 that "we have to kill and kill and kill. All day, every day."

When I was in Gaza, I saw a little boy no more than nine years old whose hands and part of his face had been blown off from a booby-trapped can of food that soldiers had left behind for Gaza's starving children. I later learned that they had also left poisoned food for people in Shujaiyya, and in the 1980s and '90s, Israeli soldiers had left booby-trapped toys in southern Lebanon that exploded when excited children picked them up.

The harm they do is diabolical, and yet they expect you to believe they are the victims. Invoking Europe's Holocaust and screaming antisemitism, they expect you to suspend fundamental human reason to believe that the daily sniping of children with so-called "kill shots" and the bombing of entire neighborhoods that bury families alive and wipe out whole bloodlines is self-defense.

They want you to believe that a man who had not eaten a thing in over 72 hours, who kept fighting even when all he had was one functioning arm, that this man was motivated by some innate savagery and irrational hatred or jealousy of Jews, rather than the indomitable yearning to see his people free in their own homeland.

It's clear to me that we're not here to debate whether Israel is an apartheid or genocidal state. This debate is ultimately about the worth of Palestinian lives; about the worth of our schools, research centers, books, art, and dreams; about the worth of the homes we worked all our lives to build and which contain the memories of generations; about the worth of our humanity and our agency; the worth of our bodies and ambitions.

Because if the roles were reversed—if Palestinians had spent the last eight decades stealing Jewish homes, expelling, oppressing, imprisoning, poisoning, torturing, raping and killing Jews; if Palestinians had killed [an estimated 30,000[1] in 2024] Jews in one year, targeted their journalists, their thinkers, their healthcare workers, their athletes, their artists, bombed every Israeli hospital, university, library, museum, cultural center, synagogue, and simultaneously set up an observation platform where people came to watch their slaughter as if a tourist attraction;

if Palestinians had corralled Jews by the hundreds of thousands into flimsy tents, bombed them in so-called safe zones, burned them alive, cut off their food, water, and medicine;

if Palestinians made Jewish children wander barefoot with empty pots; made them gather the flesh of their parents into plastic bags; made them bury their siblings, cousins, and friends; made them sneak out from their tents in the middle of the night to sleep on their parents' graves; made them pray for death just to join their families and not be alone in this terrible world anymore, and terrorized them so utterly that their children lose their hair, lose their memory, lose their minds, and made those as young as four and five years old die of heart attacks;

if we mercilessly forced their NICU [neonatal intensive care unit] babies to die, alone in hospital beds, crying until they could cry no more, dead and decomposed in the same spot;

if Palestinians used wheat-flour aid trucks to lure starving Jews, then opened fire on them when they gathered to collect a day's bread;

if Palestinians finally allowed a food delivery into a shelter with hungry Jews, then set fire to the entire shelter and the aid truck before anyone could taste the food;

if a Palestinian sniper bragged about blowing out 42 Jewish kneecaps in one day as one Israeli soldier did in 2019;

if a Palestinian admitted to CNN that he ran over hundreds of Jews with his tank, their squished flesh lingering in the tank treads;

if Palestinians were systematically raping Jewish doctors, patients, and other captives with hot metal rods, jagged and electrified sticks, and fire extinguishers, sometimes raping to death, as happened with Dr. Adnan Al-Bursh and others;

if Jewish women were forced to give birth in filth, get C-sections or leg amputations without anesthesia; if we destroyed their children then decorated our tanks with their toys;

if we killed or displaced their women then posed in their lingerie

...

if the world were watching the livestreamed, systematic annihilation of Jews in real time, there would be no debating whether that constituted terrorism or genocide.

And yet two Palestinians—myself and Mohammad el-Kurd—showed up here to do just that, enduring the indignity of debating those who think our only life choices should be to leave our homeland, submit to their supremacy, or die politely and quietly.

But you would be wrong to think that I came to convince you of anything. The house resolution, though well-meaning and appreciated, is of little consequence in the midst of this holocaust of our time.

I came in the spirit of Malcolm X and Jimmy Baldwin, both of whom stood here and in Cambridge before I was born, facing finely dressed, well-spoken monsters who harbored the same supremacist ideologies as Zionism—these notions of entitlement and privilege, of being divinely favored, blessed, or chosen.

I'm here for the sake of history. To speak to generations not yet born and for the chronicles of this extraordinary time where the carpet bombing of defenseless Indigenous societies is legitimized.

I'm here for my grandmothers, both of whom died as penniless refugees while foreign Jews lived in their stolen homes.

And I also came to speak directly to Zionists here and everywhere.

We let you into our homes when your own countries tried to murder you and everyone else turned you away. We fed and clothed you, gave you shelter, and we shared the bounty of our land with you, and when the time was ripe, you kicked us out of our own homes and homeland, then you killed and robbed and burned and looted our lives.

You carved out our hearts because it is clear you do not know how to live in the world without dominating others.

You have crossed all lines and nurtured the most vile of human impulses, but the world is finally glimpsing the terror we have endured at your hands for so long, and they are seeing the reality of who you are, who you've always been. They watch in utter astonishment the sadism, the glee, the joy, and pleasure with which you conduct, watch, and cheer the daily details of breaking our bodies, our minds, our future, our past.

But no matter what happens from here, no matter what fairy-tales you tell yourself and tell the world, you will never truly belong to that land. You will never understand the sacredness of the olive trees, which you've been cutting down and burning for decades just to spite us and to break our hearts a little more. No one native to that land would dare do such a thing to the olives. No one who belongs to that region would ever bomb or destroy such ancient heritage as Baalbek or Bittir, or destroy ancient cemeteries as you destroy ours, like the Anglican cemetery in Jerusalem or the resting place of ancient Muslim scholars and warriors in Maamanillah. Those who come from that land do not desecrate the dead; that's why my family for centuries were the caretakers of the Jewish cemetery in the Mount of Olives, as labors of faith and care, for what we know is part of our ancestry and story.

Your ancestors will always be buried in your actual homelands of Poland, Ukraine, and elsewhere around the world from whence you came. The mythos and folklore of the land will always be alien to you.

You will never be literate in the sartorial language of the thobes we wear, that sprang from the land through our foremothers over centuries—every motif, design, and pattern speaking to the secrets of local lore, flora, birds, rivers, and wildlife.

What your real estate agents call in their high-priced listings "old Arab home" will always hold in their stones the stories and memories of our ancestors who built them. The ancient photos and paintings of the land will never contain you.

You will never know how it feels to be loved and supported by those who have nothing to gain from you, and in fact, everything to lose. You will never know the feeling of masses all over the world pouring into the streets and stadiums to chant and sing for your freedom; and it is not because you are Jewish, as you try to make the world believe, but because you are depraved violent colonizers who think your Jewishness entitles you to the home my grandfather and his brothers built with their own hands—on lands that had been in our family for centuries. It is because Zionism is a blight on Judaism and indeed on humanity.

You can change your names to sound more relevant to the region and you can pretend falafel and hummus and zaatar are your ancient cuisines, but in the recesses of your being, you will always feel the sting of this epic forgery and theft. That's why even the drawings of our children, hung on walls at the UN or in a hospital ward, send your leaders and lawyers into hysteric meltdowns.

You will not erase us, no matter how many of us you kill and kill and kill, all day every day. We are not the rocks Chaim Weizmann thought you could clear from the land. We are its very soil. We are her rivers and her trees and her stories, because all of that was nurtured by our bodies and our lives over millennia of continuous, uninterrupted habitation of that patch of earth between the Jordan and Mediterranean waters. From our Canaanite, our Hebrew, our Philistine, and our Phoenician ancestors, to every conqueror or pilgrim who came and went, who married or raped, loved, enslaved, converted between religions, settled or prayed in our land, leaving pieces of themselves in our bodies and our heritage, the fabled, tumultuous stories of that land are quite literally in our DNA. You cannot kill or propagandize that away, no matter what death technology you use or what Hollywood and corporate media arsenals you deploy.

Someday, your impunity and arrogance will end. Palestine will be free; she will be restored to her multi-religious, multi-ethnic pluralistic glory; we will restore and expand the trains that run from Cairo to Gaza to Jerusalem, Haifa, Tripoli, Beirut, Damascus, Amman, Kuwait, Sanaa, and so on; we will put an end to the Zionist

American war machine of domination, expansion, extraction, pollution, and looting.

... and you will either leave, or you will finally learn to live with others as equals.

CHAPTER SIX

Fighting for the Congo[1]

Maurice Carney, Brother Passy, Kwame Wilburg, Claude Gatebuke, Dr. Ikema Ojore, BPM interview by Kalonji Changa and Rev. Keyanna Jones Moore

Kalonji Changa: [Given] what's going on over in Goma [a city in the Democratic Republic of Congo (DRC)], we wanted to talk to the experts [and] invited some brothers to talk about the Congo. Maurice, give us an overview of what's going on in the Congo, in Goma in particular … . Why [should] the world be outraged and support the people of Goma [seeking] peace and freedom.[2]

Maurice Carney: Thank you, brother. For people to understand what's going on today in Goma, we have to put it in the context of a 30-year war of aggression and plunder by U.S. allies Rwanda and Uganda. [This is a war] with the full backing of the United States and other European powers: arms, finance, training, intelligence, also diplomatic and political cover.[3]

Over 30 years, a war of aggression and plunder has ebbed and flowed. Since 2021 we've seen an acute rise in the pursuit of territory in Eastern Congo, primarily on the part of the Rwandan president, Paul Kagame.[4] They've occupied land almost the size of Rwanda itself. And in the process of occupying land [that is] mineral-rich land at that. According to the United Nations [UN], they've occupied "Rubaya," which is the largest coltan mine[5] in the region. In occupying the land, at the same time, they've encircled the city of Goma. Goma is a capital city of North Kivu, it has about 2 million people. To the east of Goma, you have Rwanda; and to the south, you have Lake Kivu, and it's been completely encircled.

What we've seen over the weekend [January 25, 2025] is an effort on the part of Rwandan soldiers and its militia group, the M23 [March 23 Movement], to enter into Goma and to capture the city ... after taking about every existing route coming out of Goma. Whether you're talking about fuel or food, that means that the city is being starved out. At the moment there's no electricity or internet access. Potable water or drinkable water is limited at best, and it's also the space of some of the largest displacement camps in the east of the Congo, because when the Rwandan soldiers, and the M23 militia occupied those villages or those towns outside of Goma, the people rushed out. They left, and went into Goma and settled in displacement camps.

One camp, for example, called Bulengo, has about 800,000 people. What is happening now, since the M23 and the Rwandan soldiers have tried to enter into Goma, the people in displacement camps are being driven into the city itself, which makes the situation even more precarious. Not only for those, for the displaced communities, but also the residents of Goma itself.

Changa: Passy, you're in the DRC, what's it looking like from your vantage point?

Passy: We are in Kinshasa, but we are in contact with brothers, with folks in Goma. The situation is very complicated after the death of the governor, who was assassinated on the front line, and the division of rebels and militias.

They haven't taken the airport yet. The Congolese army is still controlling the airports with the support of the,[6] you know, militaries and the MONUSCO.[7] Inside Goma, Wazalendo[8] militias and resistance are still fighting and trying to control the national radio and television. The Deputy Governor of Goma went to [the city of] Bukavu.

Bukavu is the neighboring province, next to North Kivu. Soldiers, military personnel ran away. There is regret and anxiety among soldiers on the ground. There is a problem of electricity and water, like brother Maurice said, and no one is leaving the house. The population is starving. There's been a number of demonstrations, especially in Bukavu, to support militaries on the front. The government is still supporting, declaring that the population has to trust in them. Although, the people are suffering.

We also saw the attacks of the Wazalendo, this is the native resistance who attacked the Gisenyi, Rubavu, who saw this province next to Goma, Rwandan province, they attacked. They attacked some random populations. So, they are surrounded.

There are still attacks inside Goma, in the avenues, and it is very complex. The M23 rebels thought that this could be an easy victory. But we are all mobilized. In social media, and on the ground, we are trying to resist. We have the morals that we should fight. This fight will be long. It is popular. We will not let them control us and take our lands. We are connected to that land. So, we're together. We are really encouraging the people, our soldiers, our brothers to continue and to rely on our efforts.

Changa: Kwame, working with Friends of Congo, there's been all eyes on that region. What is the importance of Goma to Rwanda, and not only Rwanda, but also Western governments, the Europeans, etc.? There's a lot at stake. Why is that particular region so important? Are other forces involved?

Kwame Wilburg: Yes. This is a critical time as you know. I am glad to be honest with you comrades. As Passy mentioned, the Goma airport has not fallen. This is significant ... [due to the] infrastructure that MONUSCO [the United Nations Organization Stabilization Mission in the Democratic Republic of the Congo, established by the UN Security Council] and other forces are able to deploy. So, just the strategic importance of that. Flying out of Goma, you see a massive operation with elements of the UN—of MONUSCO close to that airport. There are tremendous amounts of resources critical for fighting this battle. As much as we talk about mineral resources and territory, there are people's lives!

When we went there in 2022, Goma had about 2 million people. I've heard that the numbers have literally doubled. It's the kind of carnage of armies fighting each other and seizing land and holding prisoners of war. I've heard, I hope some of it is not true—people have been beheaded. The level of carnage. Centering the significance of Goma is not only in the mineral strategic resources, it's the human lives, the tremendous dehumanization and cost that brings back the specter of what happened in Rwanda back in 1994.

Centering that human tragedy there, and the scale of human international resources that's needed to support it, because the Congolese government has literally failed to protect the Congolese people or work in the interest of them. This area is being destabilized. One might remember that during the anti-apartheid struggle, how South Africa destabilized, disrupted the so-called frontline states, the kind of chaos that Rwanda is creating there. And of course, then that provides access to the tremendous mineral resources, in the area. Like I said, we think about them getting the resources but, we should also not dismiss the talk about annexation, the talk about seizing and holding territory. Because for all intents and purposes, the M23 has been able to hold territory.

There was a recent conversation with Kampala in Uganda and Kinshasa about road access to move resources, minerals out of eastern DRC, to export them either to Uganda or to the Indian Ocean. And that Kagame felt that he was being eclipsed, because now remember Uganda and Rwanda were pretty much on the same page in terms of some of the chaos that's being created. But, if I'm not mistaken, I think this is an important point, I don't know if maybe Maurice or Claude could lean in on this, that might have been part of what might have triggered Kagame feeling, 'Hey, wait a minute, Uganda is going to be dominating these resources at this time.'

Changa: Claude, in previous discussions we talked about the history of Rwanda. Outsiders, folks will look and say well "You have two African countries warring, what's the problem?" I want you to walk us back a little bit. You're born in Rwanda, right? You told us about the different atrocities that took place in the 1990s: how you and your mother were forced to dig your own graves. Give us some context about Rwanda, and why this is not just an "African-on-African" squabble.

Claude Gatebuke: Thank you. I appreciate that question. I think it's important. It is true that often when people see these conflicts and this type of carnage, and it's not just a simple conflict. Conflict is a watered-down term, honestly, to put it that way. When they see this type of aggression, they think, "Oh, this is African tribalism." This is "African-on-African," "Black-on-Black crime"—the typical framing of these types of atrocities.

What is happening in the Congo? If it was recognized as "African country fighting another African country," that will be a step forward in being honest about the narrative. The M23 is actually the Rwandan army invading the Congo and the Ugandan army invading the Congo. Those two countries invaded the Congo, and they have, over the years, come up with a whole number of so-called rebel groups, these proxy militias that fight their wars and occupy the Congo. I think the recognition is really important that number one, this is recognized as a war of aggression from both Rwanda and Uganda into the Congo. The second thing is, there is a tendency to always frame this as an attack on Eastern Congo. Right now, if somebody was to ask most people, what side of Ukraine was attacked by Russia? Do we know whether it was east or south or whatever? No, it's a country that has been invaded. Even one inch ... east, west, south. Rwanda and Uganda have invaded Congo....

But they do not have the resources to actually invade the Congo on their own. This isn't "African tribalism," although Paul Kagame and Museveni, Uganda's president, would like to claim it as a war, a war of tribalism, and these are like internal groups to the Congo that are just staging an internal self-defense fight. This is incorrect. This is an invasion. These two countries are two of the poorest countries in the world. They do not have the resources to actually invade another country. They do not manufacture weapons. They don't even have budgets that would be able to purchase the amounts of weapons required to fight these wars. They are supported by the United States, United Kingdom, European Union. These nations back financially [militarism and invasions]; there's always one or two excuses to fund Rwanda's military. [What] Rwanda's military and Uganda's military are doing and have done is to serve in Central Africa, in the Great Lakes Region of Africa, over the whole continent, and as far as the Caribbean—in Haiti. Rwandan soldiers and Ugandan soldiers serve as local mercenaries for Western countries and for Western multinationals, where the U.S. will no longer need to send their soldiers to a place like Somalia, for example.

Right now, when it comes to exploiting all reserves in Mozambique, Rwandan troops are down in Cabo Delgado to secure resources for French companies, in the parts of Congo near the border with Uganda, Ugandan troops are there to secure resources for French oil companies. When it comes to mines, Ugandan and Rwandan troops are occupying parts of Congo to provide access for international companies—especially those on the Toronto Stock Market—Canadian companies along with American companies, European companies in a variety of countries, including Switzerland, France, Belgium, and the UK, to secure those mines.

So, these are local mercenaries that are doing the bidding for not only Western countries, but, you know, for Western countries' interests in terms of an imperialist expansion and occupation, but also for Western multinationals to extract these resources. So, this now ties back to the Rwandan genocide. What Rwanda has used as an excuse to invade the Congo is initially, they said that, excuse me— let's maybe roll it back and kind of work the timeline forward.

In the early 1980s, Museveni, Uganda's president, lost an election in Uganda. Then he started a war which lasted years. They committed mass atrocities, including rape and horrible sexual violence, amputations and beheadings—the things that you're hearing that are happening in Goma today. This was the practice ground in Uganda. In 1986, he won. Some of his fighters, included Paul Kagame and many exiled Rwandans. In 1990, a group from the military, from the Ugandan military, formed a rebel group—the same way they're doing it in the Congo—and invaded Rwanda. So, basically Uganda invaded Rwanda in 1990. This is the four-year war with major atrocities again, with this group led by Paul Kagame, the RPF [Rwanda Patriotic Front], which is in power in Rwanda today committing major atrocities: sexual violence, torture, atrocities. This four-year war led to the genocide in Rwanda.

Then Paul Kagame won, and at the end of the genocide claimed to actually stop the genocide. Then two years later, this is '94, two years later, in '96—this is almost 30 years ago—he invaded the Congo with the pretext of going after those who committed genocide in Rwanda. But you always wondered, why is it, if they were going after those who committed genocide in Rwanda, one of the things that they did was the time of their attacks ... the time when mining or harvesting was done, and they went right to the stocks of resources. Of course, they massacred hundreds of thousands of people from Rwanda in the refugee camps. We've talked about that on this show, and they caused, they massacred thousands and thousands, hundreds of thousands of Congolese. And this invasion, both by Rwanda and Uganda, by the way, they both invaded Congo at the same time, has led to the death of more than 6 million Black people on the continent of Africa.

When it comes to imperialism, neocolonialism, occupation and white supremacy and anti-black racism, it looks so much better when you have a mercenary, a Black mercenary like Paul Kagame and a Black mercenary like Yoweri Museveni, who is doing the killing. It looks like Black-on-Black crime. You know it's nice for the optics. These are servants of the West. These are the local plantation managers for the West, the local mercenaries for the West who do their bidding all over the world.

Why has the world been so silent for the last 30 years? Prior to the technological advances in social media opening up to where everybody has a voice to go around the world, news was filtered through corporate media. Everything was filtered through the gatekeepers, the academics and people who basically align with these Western governments and go with the Western narrative of Paul Kagame, president of Rwanda, being a hero [while] he is mass murdering Africans. Yoweri Museveni, president of Uganda, being a hero, because he's mass murdering Africans.[9] What we have in Goma is just one more of many attacks in the Congo by Rwanda and Uganda with the support of Western imperial powers.

Remember when the war in Ukraine started and Russia invaded Ukraine, there were all these sanctions? We haven't seen sanctions to that degree when it comes to Rwanda. There were sanctions.[10] But you see the double standard in the complicity by Western imperial powers, they don't apply the same rules when it comes to the Congolese. This isn't to say that they have the high moral ground to impose these sanctions, but it is also to call out the hypocrisy of allowing such atrocities to take place. This is similar to what is happening in Palestine, with Israel. The Israel apartheid regime, invading, and going into Gaza and committing genocide and actually continuing to be awarded with billions of dollars in weapons and money from U.S. tax dollars, from U.S. taxpayers. What is happening in Goma, and in Congo in general, is connected to us by us just being taxpayers, and also being consumers. Every single one of us has devices powered by resources that come out of the Congo. And so, this is a global issue, it's not a local issue.

You were asking "How is it connected to the Rwandan genocide?" Kwame was also asking about the regional connections and resources. The Goma airport is right near the UN base. "M23 rebels," the Rwandan troops, have killed UN troops. Remember what happened in Sierra Leone? That's usually the last straw. When the rebels in Sierra Leone started going after UN troops, that's when it all escalated. What I think is happening today is that Kagame is doing what he's doing because he's being left out of the deal with Uganda. I think it's an escalation to create some kind of negotiating leverage. It also comes back to the incompetence of the Congolese officials who today have not shown a level of seriousness needed to deal with this issue.

I have a proposal. The Congo, Congolese government, needs to close its borders with Rwanda and Uganda. I have an uncle on the Rwanda side and an auntie on the Congo side. It's walking distance, the borders are porous. [Closing the borders] will stop commerce, the smuggling of resources from going from inside of Congo to inside of Rwanda to be transported ... into Uganda to be sold on the global market. Flights from [Rwanda and Uganda] will not ... [benefit the Congo people who] are being slaughtered. It will escalate because they care about their money, shutting down the borders and shutting down commerce. You're not shutting down the people who are walking; you're shutting down the trucks that are transporting things. When these companies, their stocks, their profits, start to get hit, the international community will start to act, not because they care about the human beings that are being killed. Obviously, it's almost useless to appeal to their morality and sympathy, but they will do it because it is hurting their pockets.

Changa: An Atlanta politician has strong ties and has a relationship with Paul Kagame and that regime. Can you speak on this particular Atlanta politician who's been at the center of ... on the side of building Cop City ... and who has investments with Paul Kagame?

Gatebuke: This is the none other than Andrew Young [former civil rights aide to Rev. Martin Luther King, Jr.]. He is not only close with Paul Kagame; he also has lobbied for Kagame, and done this at the U.S. federal level. He also has promoted business opportunities for Kagame, the mass murderer. This is the person that I called the "Hitler of Africa." More than 6 million innocent lives taken in the African continent. The same Andrew Young that was a part of the Civil Rights Movement, the same Andrew Young that was a mayor of Atlanta, the same Andrew Young that was U.S. ambassador to the UN [and U.S. Congressman]. That Andrew Young. Over ten years ago, Paul Kagame had one of his pep rallies—they call them 'Rwanda Days'—in Atlanta. One of the speakers at the event was Andrew Young; he seemed surprised that there was a protest against Kagame in Atlanta. That politician is supporting Cop Cities.

Rev. Keyanna Jones Moore: No surprise about Andrew Young. No surprise that the Georgia International Law Enforcement Exchange, which imports and exports violence from places like Israel and other places that have very bad human rights records, is housed within the Andrew Young School of Public Policy at Georgia State University. No surprise that the same Andrew Young was ambassador to the United Nations that stands by and allows these atrocities to happen.

When we think about the global context, and we make the connection between genocide everywhere, and if we are thinking of what was going on in Palestine even before October 7, 2023, Israel was going into Palestine and bombing near UN buildings. They were bombing actual UN buildings. They were sniping people who are coming in and out of these UN buildings. Many times, even schools run by the UN were subject to invasion by Israeli Occupation Forces, and they would just kidnap the children and hold them for as long as they wanted. This all predates October 7, 2023.

But when we think about the United Nations as a body, the International Criminal Court or the International Court of Justice, we know that right now there are warrants for a certain prime minister that is responsible for genocide, but they're not being executed because of the support of the United States, the United Kingdom and other Western forces. When we think about the atrocities occurring in the Congo, Rwanda and Uganda have been empowered by these same Western forces, U.S., UK, and other Western forces that profit. Media companies are profiting: Google, Microsoft, Amazon. Partnerships between Google and Amazon make it so that the Democratic Republic of the Congo is exploited for its natural resources, and labor, in particular, the child's labor.

When we look at the way that Israel has murdered, pillaged, and the genocide that's occurred in Palestine, we saw a targeted attack on children. We know that the population of the Democratic Republic of Congo is heavily youth-centric. We know that a large part of this population is not even 16 years old yet. So, if you are going to take out an entire people as you are attacking the older people, we are committing genocide, right? Let's be serious. When people are told to evacuate, those displacement camps become concentration camps, where people are murdered. They are murdering the adults there, but also murdering children in the mines. You're murdering the children because they won't turn into soldiers. You're murdering the children as they seek to fend for themselves, to get food, to get clean water, all the things that have been done in Palestine, we see the same playbook. You're withholding food. You're withholding water. You are using sexual violence as a tool of war. The forces that are behind this will continue to support Rwanda, Uganda, and they are not being held accountable. The United States Congress is not being held accountable. The UK is not being held accountable. Other Western European countries that support this also are not being held accountable.

At this point, I'm always asking: When are the rest of us really going to stand up and put a stop to it? When are the rest of us going to decide that we are going to pack out the UN at the Human Rights Committee? When are the rest of us going to stand up and say: "You know what? I don't care about your warrants ICC.* If nothing is happening, we are not going to let there be peace in these streets." There can't be rest in these streets. When are we going to show up? We really need to show up for our brothers and sisters in Congo. Because we know that it's not just the Congo. We know what's happening in Sudan. We know what's going on in Haiti. What do we see? We keep seeing the proliferation of Western forces taking other Africans to do their bidding. When are we, as Africans, going to say enough is enough?

Changa: It's a call to action: definitely appreciate that. Ikemba, any words?

Ojore: I appreciate sister Keyanna, that call for action, and definitely the information on the Congo, because its [devastation has] been going on for a long time, and we can go further back than the 1990s. I appreciate what Sister Keyanna said, too, in regards to what's happening throughout Africa, because these stories don't get media attention. Central African Republic is a place that I like to look at; and I'm always looking for those stories. That's another place that we need to be paying attention to.
South Africa has sent troops into the Congo. China has interest in the Congo, and some [investment] of the largest mining companies in Congo. Readings suggest that the Chinese are smuggling gold bars out of Congo. China has economic interests? Who are some of these players in the DRC? I read that Uganda was part of the Alliance to push back M23. How true is that?

Gatebuke: I think that question goes back to what Kwame mentioned: the Congolese government has fumbled this in the way that they have acted. In 2013, Uganda was a part of the coalition to sup-

---

* International Criminal Court.

posedly stop the conflict, stop the M23. It was in 2022, when the Congo joined the East African Community [EAC]. And ... there were troops from the East African Community that were sent into the Congo. Already that was a problem, and the problem is, part of the East African Community, our countries are actually invading the Congo. Rwanda and Uganda are part of the East African Community.

So, there was objection to Rwandan troops being a part of that group of troops, so Rwandan troops were not included, at least not officially. Ugandan troops who invaded the Congo, who had actually facilitated the taking of the border town of Muna, Ghana, in recent times, at that time by the M23, were included in this group of troops. It was one of the dumbest, dumbest endeavors of allowing troops to come into your country, and including the invaders who actually come in there. And one of the things that the Congolese people have is resilience. I mean, for years they've been killed, maimed, enslaved, and they continue to fight. You know, the practice of amputating people was widely practiced in the Congo, and the Congolese never back down. It's one of the places where nobody has ever really been able to control the whole territory in totality with an iron fist, regardless of whether it was colonialism, dictatorship, invaders, no one has been able to do this because of the Congolese people's resilience. So, the Congolese people, they were just relentless. They protested against it, until officially those troops were sent out of the Congo.

Now, the South African troops are part of a UN brigade. This was also brought in to fight back [against] the M23. In previous times, in 2012, is when, basically, Rwanda and Uganda's invasion of Congo was renamed as the M23. [They] got rid of the previous names ... and they've continued to evolve and change those names. During that time, a number of things happened. A UN brigade of Malawi, Tanzanian and South African troops actually engaged in a fight against the M23. There was some international action where the U.S. started by withholding a portion of military aid to Rwanda [$200,000 in 2012; in FY 2023, the U.S. provided $175m to Rwanda]. They withheld basically one person's salary [in the federal government], that's what it's equivalent to. That started a domino effect, where European countries started withholding millions of dollars from the Rwandan government. Within months, the M23 completely disappeared, it went into Uganda, and then it came back in 2022, they reincarnated in the Congo.[11] Most of the people who fled from Congo, from the M23, went to Uganda.

That wasn't the first time that Uganda had invaded Congo. The first invasion of the Congo in this period started almost thirty years ago, in 1996. The same time that Rwandan troops invaded Congo, the Ugandan troops were their partners in crime. These are criminals without borders. There are Doctors Without Borders, Journalists Without Borders, Reporters Without Borders, also we've got "Criminals Without Borders." These Criminals Without Borders, from Uganda and in Rwanda, went into the Congo together. This has been happening for years. Because of the incompetence of the Congolese government, there are times when you would think that Uganda is actually an ally of the Congo. It might be an ally of the Congolese leaders, but it is not an ally of the Congolese people; it's actually one of the butchers of the Congolese people. During a previous administration, there were times when that administration would strike deals with Paul Kagame of Rwanda and his murderous, criminal, genocidal regime, and Kagame would send their troops into the Congo.

These countries, today, deny being a part of the invasion of Congo, especially Rwanda in the 1990s. This has happened before also: there was a time when, for years, Rwanda was saying, "No, this is a Congo issue, we don't have our troops in the Congo, do not ask us about what's happening in the Congo, that's an internal problem," just like they're pretending today. So, they say this for years and years, and then one day, they held a ceremony to celebrate Rwandan troops returning from the Congo. Troops that supposedly were never there, that they denied were there the whole time, they actually had a ceremony like they had planes landing and like a whole procession of soldiers. The denial of the fact that Rwanda and Uganda are occupying Congo has been going on for a long time. Uganda is trying to be slick in trying to transform the narrative into, "We are partners, we are invited, we're doing this at the invitation of the Congolese government." I keep repeating about the incompetence of the Congolese government, but at the same time, it's no excuse for the invaders, the local plantation managers, the local mercenaries, to go into the Congo and commit the atrocities that they are committing. It is no excuse for the international community to arm, fund and defend the invaders of Congo and profit from the resources of the Congo.

Changa: Maurice, for Friends of the Congo, what's the plan? I almost feel like a coward, because I can't do anything to help. I recognize the folks on the screen as fighters—while we are working on this broadcast right now, there's war, there's blood being shed. Someone just caught a bullet, someone is being raped, someone, somewhere, is being pillaged while we're doing this platform, while we're comfortable. It's not a knock on anyone; unfortunately, we're doing more than most. . . . We can't just hop on the plane and head to Rwanda. We can't even get off the block sometimes to deal with the BS that's happening. I am a realist.

Carney: Claude said it earlier, right? It's not just a local issue. The reason why that war of aggression and plunder is able to continue locally is because of the support that these agents of neocolonialism offer here in Washington, or in Atlanta. So, there's a role for us where we are, because this is not just something that's happening in Goma or North Kivu or the Great Lakes. It's happening there because of what is happening in Washington, DC, in Brussels, because of London and Paris. So, it's important for us to understand the nature of the war of aggression and plunder.

Folks want to help: go to freecongo.org. Rev. Keyanna talked about getting in the streets, folks are going to be in the streets tomorrow, and in New York at the UN. Stay up to date. Hit us up on Instagram @congofriends or Twitter @congofriends. In DC, we're going to be in the streets in front of the Rwandan embassy. Kwame and brothers and sisters in Atlanta are planning something there. So be in solidarity with us as we get in the streets. Even if you're not able to make it, let people know: "Hey, there is pressure being put on the Rwandan government, UN, U.S. government, so it's vital for us to continue to do that."

In terms of a plan, the first thing is to support the people. We're working with our partners on the ground. They're in the displacement camps. A displacement camp called Bulengo has about 800,000 people, they are being bombed. People had to evacuate, relocate. We had to mobilize resources right and get them on the ground so that people can move, get food, build their own shelter. That's the first concern: make sure that our people are protected. We mobilize resources so that we can get information coming out to journalists in our network. We would have loved to have one of them on with you today, but [he's] been out of communication for the last ten hours, so we don't know whether he's dead or alive. His last communication was: "Hey, there are bullets flying through my door; and I gotta take cover, I can't even go to the UN because they don't protect journalists." So, to the extent to which we can, we support the people. We also have to understand the nature and the scope of this operation. It's not just a military operation. The United States puts hundreds of billions, trillions of dollars in their military? [As if] that's not enough ... they also launch a propaganda campaign and say, "Hey, you know Iraq has weapons of mass destruction," and they have to get media in line in order to justify their wars.

The central question for us, all of us, in mobilizing around the Congo, is that we have to rally around the people who are fighting against imperialist forces that want to continue to plunder the Congo. Joe Biden went to Angola in December 2024, he was going to trumpet the Lobito Corridor, that line that runs from the heart of the Congo out to Lobito Port in Angola, that goes out faster—two or three times faster than they've been going out before. So, when we talk about Congo and the heart of Africa, this is really what's at stake. Kagame is an aspect of it. We are talking about a space in the heart of the African continent where Frantz Fanon said, "The fate, the fate of all of us, is at stake, right there, in the heart of Africa." That's what Fanon said—toward African revolution. So, that's what we need to understand as an African people. We need to understand what Fanon understood. We need to understand what Malcolm understood. We need to understand what Kwame Nkrumah understood when he wrote *The Challenge of Congo*.[12]

Our fate is tied up there, and the extent to which the Congolese are successful is the same extent to which Africa will be successful. That's not me talking, that's Ernesto "Che" Guevara.[13] He went to the Congo. Fidel Castro sent him in 1965. Che stated: "This is the front lines of the battle against colonialism…. I am gonna be here with the Congolese to fight." That's a revolutionary. Che said that the Congo's challenge is not just the Congolese challenge, but it's a worldwide concern.

Think about the centrality of the Congo, the so-called "green energy transition" to combating the climate crisis being a part of the second largest rainforest in the world, sequestering more carbon than all of the tropical rainforests combined. Home to the largest tropical peat lands. Producing minerals that are vital to EVs—the electric vehicles we drive; the batteries in our cell phones, etc. It's just critical to the planet. If we're concerned about all of these things as, just as human beings, you know, not even Pan-Africanists or Africanists, just as human beings, we really need to be engaged and assure that the oppressed masses of the Congo triumph. Triumph in the sense that they control their land, they control their wealth, they control their resources, and ultimately control their affairs for the benefit of Congo and for the benefit of Africa and the African world. So that's what's at stake.

In the case of Rwanda, it has a massive propaganda campaign, not to justify its war against the Congolese people, but to actually cleanse the crimes that it's committing in the Congo, to actually cleanse the atrocities that it's committing in the Congo. And in doing that, they connect with a range of people. Congo officials have invited entertainers, especially Black entertainers, to Rwanda: Kendrick Lamar; Dave Chappelle; John Legend [are] planning to go [Legend performed in Kigali, Rwanda on February 21, 2025]. We're saying, "Hey, hit up John Legend, and say "You are covering for a war criminal!" What Claude called the "Hitler of Africa." We need to put pressure on those entertainers, the entire NBA [National Basketball Association] [ignores war atrocities]. ESPN [Entertainment and Sports Programming Network] did an investigative piece on how Kagame is using sports— basically "sports washing" the crimes he is committing in Rwanda and in the Congo. We need to be hitting up the basketball players, [telling them] that [atrocities are] happening: "Do you know what's going on and how your sports league is being used to cover crimes against Black people, in the Congo?" We need a Colin Kaepernick*... for a host of issues, not just the Congo.

These are some of the things that we're saying to people that they can be a part of if they want to be in the comfort of their homes and social media, you know, use your iPhone. Use that coltan† from the Congo to hit these folks up and say, "Hey, you know, you're covering for this guy." Follow us on @congofriends on Instagram. Hit us up at freecongo.org so that you can, know, get involved, take some action and be a part of the larger movement.

This isn't a question of a movement against Kagame. He is just the latest version of the plunder and the ravaging of the Congo. Kagame is a "Johnny-come-lately." The Congo has been set up for plunder and ravaging by imperialists. It was founded for plunder.[14] This is continuing. And when the one amazing Congolese figure, along with his comrades, rose up to disrupt that plunder, right, and Patrice Lumumba in 1960 was elected as prime minister, the United States mounted the largest covert action in the world: overthrow and assassinate Lumumba to assure that plunder continues to this very day.

Changa: Maurice just said, "everywhere is Congo." Wherever you at, pick up the fight against imperialism, pick up the fight against Zionism, pick up the fight against colonialism, pick up the fight against capitalism. And that's how we crush it on a worldwide scale. You don't have to get on a plane to go to Rwanda, the Sudan or to the Congo or to Palestine. Thank you, Maurice, Claude, Kwame, Dr. Ikemba Ojore, and Brother Passy. We need to have more of these roundtable discussions about imperialism to stay updated on what's going on. Many people don't know about the Congo. Salute to you all. Hands off the Congo. Run the czars, around the planet, out of town.

---

*   U.S. civil rights organizer and former professional football quarterback, who would be barred due to his anti-racist activism.
†   Coltan is a mineral used in cellphones.

PART III
COUNTER MOVES

CHAPTER SEVEN

The Prisoner Human Rights Movement [PHRM]: 2025 Nobel Letter and the Agency of PHRM

Joy James with Silicon Valley De-Bug Organization

January 31, 2025

To: The Norwegian Nobel Committee Members: ...
RE: Prisoner Human Rights Movement (PHRM) Organization Nomination for The Nobel Peace Prize.

Norwegian Nobel Institute,
I submit my nomination of the organization Prisoner Human Rights Movement (PHRM) which is represented by five PHRM Representatives (candidates) for the Nobel Peace Prize based on their courageous peace efforts and hunger strikes to end indefinite solitary confinement, also known as torture, inside and beyond California prisons.

History of the Prisoner Human Rights Movement (PHRM)

The Pelican Bay State Prison-Security Housing Unit (PBSP-SHU) Short Corridor Collective / Prisoner Human Rights Movement (PHRM) Representatives include the following imprisoned human rights advocates: (1) Todd Ashker, PHRM Representative, San Luis Obispo, CA (California Men's Colony—CMC), United States; (2) Arturo Castellanos, PHRM Representative, Delano, CA (North Kern State Prison—NKSP), United States; (3) Sitawa Nantambu Jamaa (Dewberry), PHRM Representative, Oakland,

CA, United States; (4) Antonio Guillen, PHRM Representative, Florence, CO (USP Florence ADMAX, U.S. Penitentiary), USA; (5) George Franco, PHRM Representative, Vacaville, CA (California Medical Facility—CMF), USA.

Although not nominated, the ten members of the Representative Body of the Prisoner Human Rights Movement (PHRM) and Agreement to End Hostilities (AEH) should also be applauded for their work: Danny Troxell; Ronnie Yandell; Paul Redd; James Baridi Williamson; Alfred Sandoval; Louis Powell; Alex Yrigollen; Gabriel Huerta; Frank Clement; Raymond Chavo Perez; James Mario Perez.

In 2012, representatives of the PHRM housed in Pelican Bay's Short Corridor formed a historic peace effort known as the Agreement to End Hostilities (AEH), ending tensions between all racial groups in California Department of Corrections and Rehabilitation (CDCR) after five decades. In 2013, 30,000 people inside California's prison system went on a historic hunger strike to end indefinite solitary confinement in CDCR based solely on "gang" validation. . . . Prior to the *Ashker* [*Ashker v. Governor of California*] legal settlement, prisoners remained in solitary confinement indefinitely based on political ideals, art, reading literature, regional upbringing, ethnicity, family and friends. Solitary consisted of a small cell for 23 hours a day without sunlight, with one hour of exercise alone in a concrete room; and meals delivered through a small slot. PHRM Representative Sitawa Jamaa was granted medical parole in 2024, after 43 years in prison for a crime that someone else confessed to committing. In 1982, after only one year of incarceration, Sitawa was shot by a correctional officer. By 1985, Sitawa was thrown in indefinite solitary confinement for sharing George Jackson's book, *Soledad Brother* and remained there until his release into general population in 2015 with the *Ashker* settlement. Sitawa served 34 years of his 43-year sentence in solitary confinement.

In 2015, Hunger Strikers agreed to a settlement [based on] *Ashker v. Governor of California* that reformed solitary confinement in the California prisons system from a classification-based system to a behavior-based system while also ending indefinite solitary confinement. The PHRM Hunger Strikes co-led a statewide campaign that included ending or subsiding hostilities between racial groups in CDCR, solidarity efforts to end solitary confinement in county jails, including *Chavez v. County of Santa Clara*, all amounting to the greatest peace efforts in American prison history. The AEH continues to initiate policy and legislative changes, to promote peace.

Imprisoned Northern and Southern *Raza* (Chicanos-Mexicans-Latinos)—at war since the 1960s—initiated an additional cease fire policy that influenced *Raza* with a new perspective upon release, where there is focus on families in the community. In Los Angeles, a peace treaty ended 25 years of generational ingrained street racial tensions between the East Coast Crips and Florencia 13. After compassionate release, Braulio Castellano's, brother to PHRM Representative Arturo Castellanos, helped initiate peace efforts between Black and Brown that enabled young Black and Brown children and their families to travel to schools, parks, corner stores without fear of gang violence. AEH developed the conditions for peace unifying these communities. According to Sitawa Jamaa's public statement: "These brothas are still committed to the end of hostilities. And, that could carry on to the streets."

PHRM co-led civil and human rights, and social safety. Imprisoned activists organized inside, the PHRM organized with community activists outside for criminal justice reform legislation (Prop 57, SB 81, SB 1437, AB 333) to decrease California imprisonment and crime. PHRM organized and endured hunger strikes to attain significant criminal justice reforms through legislation over a decade. The *Ashker v. Governor of CA* settlement and the AEH decreased violence in prison; and on California streets. In 2006, the California prison population was overcapacity with 171,000 prisoners; in 2024, CDCR it held 90,000 people, a decrease of nearly 50%. In 2025, CDCR plans to terminate for-profit private prisons contracts with six out-of-state facilities. In 2006, the Juvenile [prison] population was at 11,000, in 2025 it dropped to 2,000. As of 2020, California's violent crime rate was 46% lower than it was in 1995. In 2023, slightly more than 3,000 people were incarcerated in California's women's prisons a decrease of about 70% in 2010.

Justification for This Nomination

... PHRM has considerable contributions to human rights struggles in carceral zones. It has skillfully navigated California prison systems to address its draconian penal institutions with decades of abuses and torture through solitary confinement.

Why PHRM Deserves the Nobel Peace Prize

PHRM deserves the Nobel Peace Prize because there is something radiant and uplifting for both the incarcerated and non-incarcerated who learn that imprisoned people have risked their mental and emotional stability and lives to advocate for humanity and peace, within environments akin to war theaters. Moving beyond survival in carceral settings, PHRM has addressed prison and state violence by imprisoned people and prison guards and administrations. Within a zone in which mental, moral, spiritual, physical integrity is often eviscerated, PHRM formed in prisons and transformed bureaucracy and brutality to in order to develop human rights protocols. PHRM cares and holds everyone accountable for their roles in inflicting violence. Their call to cease racial warfare among the incarcerated transformed penal social interactions. Their call to modify and lessen solitary confinement—where people are banned from human touch, conversation, and the natural environment—was transformational. PHRM has called for the cessation of racial animosities and prison violence—at times fueled by police/prison employees.

Security Housing Units (SHU) or solitary confinement have less harmful guidelines due to PHRM. PHRM organizes to deter SHU, death row, gang retaliations, guard brutality and beatings/chokings leading to disabilities or deaths. Under severe conditions, five central founders and members of PHRM brought law suits against the state and organized human rights protocols and infrastructure to advocate for human life and wellbeing within a zone in which people are doing life sentences for alleged or factual crimes.

Joy James

*   *   *

The above content of the letter depended upon the insights and analyses of Silicon Valley De-Bug (SVD) and discussions with Zach Kirk. Their request to send a letter to Nobel on behalf of PHRM was important and educational. Support for the California Prisoner Hunger Strikers is necessary. The hunger strikers "quote George Jackson: 'Settle your quarrels, come together, understand the reality of our situation, understand that fascism is already here' through their revolutionary [action]." PHRM is a treasure trove of organizing and fortitude under repressive prison conditions. The 2012 Agreement to End Hostilities[1] outlines the importance of reducing self-harm/group-harm and organizing for civil and human rights, and racially fueled violence.

According to the Silicon Valley De-Bug, the 30,000 hunger strikers a decade ago created human rights opportunities and made reform and resentencing laws less draconian. SVD also notes that in 2024, two human rights organizers were charged and convicted of RICO—seen as an attempt by police/prison agencies to criminalize respected members of diverse racial groups and force them into the federal prison system—to become permanent political prisoners within a penal state, that maintains fear of organizers that encourage "budding street peace."

SVD's notes how incarcerated human rights advocates and organizers worked so that *Ashker v. Governor* was first filed as a class action in 2012, as thousands of prisoners across the state of California suffered in solitary confinement in Security Housing Units (SHU). At Pelican Bay State Prison, 500 prisoners were held in the SHU for over 10 years; 78 prisoners for 20+ years. Warehoused in windowless concrete cells, nearly 24 hours a day, with no phone calls and infrequent visits, speaking through plexiglass, with few rehabilitation services and limited social interaction with others. SVD notes that organizers celebrated key victories by 2015:

#1 California solitary confinement transitioned from "a status-based system to a behavior-based system" using solitary (SHU) only if the imprisoned person was found guilty at hearing for a serious rule violation.

2. Those found guilty of gang affiliations would have access to "a two-year SHU step-down program for return to general population after serving their determinate SHU term." Those with proven gang-related activities would be transferred to a two–four-step program, with no offenses after two years they return to the general-population.

#3. California reviews all current gang-validated SHU prisoners within one year to determine release from solitary under the settlement terms.

#4. California creates a new Restricted Custody General Population Unit (RCGP) as a secure alternative to solitary confinement. RCGP people have access to educational courses, yard recreation, leisure activities, job opportunities, phone calls.

#5. Prolonged solitary confinement will allow out-of-cell time for those in the SHU.

#6. Prisoner representatives and plaintiffs' counsel and the magistrate judge monitor and implement the settlement.

CHAPTER EIGHT

The Abolition of Carceral Schooling

rosalind hampton

The word "carceral" typically refers to jails and prisons, the ideas they rely on and the ways they function. The *carceral state* is a term recognizing that jails and prisons do not function in isolation and refers to the broader network of institutions beyond prisons that practice and normalize punishment, control, and confinement.

In the beginning of the 2000s, the phrase "school-to-prison pipeline," became popular as a way to refer to how school systems push some students out of school, increasing their chances of ending up in juvenile detention centers and from there, adult prisons. According to this analysis, being pushed out of school limits youth's future education and career options, orients them toward criminalized activities and street economies, and in this way places them on a trajectory toward prison. Hundreds of research studies, articles and books have examined how education systems in the U.S. and Canada push Black, Indigenous, disabled, and poor children and youth out of schools and into prisons. Preventing, transforming, disrupting, and dismantling the school-to-prison pipeline has been a central topic of discussion for educators, policy makers, and funders. During this time, there has also been heightened attention to incidents of violence in schools, and increased funding for collaborations between local schools and police forces, including the stationing of police officers within schools. While some people believe that having police in schools increases safety and creates more positive relationships between youth and police, ample research demonstrates that the opposite is the case. Having police in schools leads to more suspensions and expulsions, and the further criminalization of especially Black and other minoritized youth.

Critiques of the idea of a school-to-prison pipeline as the dominant way of thinking about the relationships between schools and prison, show that this idea has been used to justify educational reform that in fact *maintains* carceral schooling. Notions of a school-to-prison pipeline limit understandings of the mutually reinforcing nature of schools and prisons, and fail to account for their shared foundations. Imagining the school and the prison as distinct fixed entities on opposite ends of a spectrum tends to posit schools as desirable, good places. This ignores how many of the practices of control and enclosure that we associate with contemporary prisons were foregrounded decades prior by those of public education. Getting rid of carceral schooling requires getting rid of carceral schools.

As It Was in the Beginning

> Why haven't you learned anything?
> Man, that school shit is a joke
> The same people who control the school system control
> The prison system, and the whole social system
> Ever since slavery, naw I'm sayin'?
>
> —Dead Prez, "They School," February 8, 2000

Formal education is a foundational institution of nation-state building. In what would become Canada and the United States, the first schools established in the 17th century were colonial colleges intended to train Christian missionaries and "civilize" selected Indigenous youth by teaching them Christianity and European culture and values. During this time the children of settlers were initially educated by their families at home, with the wealthiest youth returning to Britain for higher education. As the settler populations grew, colleges and universities were established by clergymen and colonial merchants (who were also the largest classes of slave owners). These schools, built on stolen Indigenous land, promoted European knowledge and ideals and developed white supremacist racial knowledges meant to justify and further imperialism, settler colonialism, and chattel slavery.

Teaching enslaved Black people to read and write was increasingly forbidden in the colonies, for fear that educated slaves would read abolitionist literature and organize rebellions. By the 19th century, slave literacy was heavily restricted or illegal in several states, although some schools were organized by (white and Black) abolitionists to teach Black people Christianity, vocational skills, and African/Black histories and culture. Attempts to deny Black people education did not prevent us from passing on knowledges through oral history, or from secretly teaching ourselves and one another literacy skills.

Publicly funded elementary schools were established for white children by the mid-19th century, while schools for Black children remained inadequately funded or without government support altogether. U.S. public schools and universities were racially segregated by law, as were schools in Nova Scotia and Ontario (then Canada West), the parts of Canada with the largest Black populations due to northern migrations of thousands of Black people from the U.S following the American Revolution in the late 18th century, and the U.S. Fugitive Slave Act of 1850. Even in parts of Canada where it was not legislated, racial segregation of schools was common practice and controlled through restricted admissions. Escalating their attempts to indoctrinate and control Indigenous peoples, 19th-century governments in Canada and the U.S. began forcibly removing Indigenous children from their families, effectively incarcerating them in government-funded boarding schools. These residential schools, most run by the Church, were sites of horrific psychological, physical, and sexual violence for over a century.

Police forces in the U.S. and Canada were developed to protect the colonial ruling classes and their assumed property rights. The "property" in question included stolen Indigenous land and enslaved Black people, who were hunted, captured, and returned to their "owners" by 18th- and 19th-century slave patrols. From these origins, the function of police has been to protect and maintain the social order through suppressing, punishing, and eliminating resistance to colonial-capitalism and white supremacy. Indigenous peoples, Black people, poor people, workers, and racialized migrants are always assumed to be threats to the white settler nation-state

CONFRONTING COUNTERINSURGENCY

project that oppresses, exploits, and kills us, and policing has always entailed disproportionate efforts to monitor, control, and contain the physical and social movement of these populations. Police are state forces of counterinsurgency.

The perceived need for cops in public schools directly coincides with racial desegregation and perceived threats to the dominant race-class order that schools are intended to uphold. In the U.S., School Resource Officer (SRO) programs emerged in the 1950s, following the legal integration of schools and increasing Black migration to the northern states. SRO programs began to be implemented in Canada in the 1970s, following changes to immigration laws and the arrival of increasing numbers of Black and other racialized / non-European immigrants, and the coinciding institutionalization of liberal multicultural education as the dominant means of managing and incorporating these groups into Canadian society. In both countries, SRO programs have been increasingly widespread since the late 1990s. While in some cases activists and educators have successfully campaigned to have SROs removed from school boards in the past decade, several of these SRO programs have more recently been reinstated. Reflecting the broader framework of community policing of which they are a part, SRO programs are rationalized as promoting positive contact and relationships between police and community members. Conversely, they are widely critiqued for disproportionately targeting Black, Indigenous, poor, disabled, and undocumented migrant children and youth for surveillance, harassment, discipline, and criminalization.

Universities in the U.S. also began to establish their own police forces during the civil rights era, prior to which security guards patrolled and protected university property from those deemed outsiders. Especially in cities with large Black populations, 20th-century university administrators sought to maintain (the whiteness and) control of neighborhoods surrounding university campuses. To reassure white middle-class residents of the lasting value of their property—their homes, schools, and their whiteness itself—universities invested in programs of "urban renewal," expanding their campuses and displacing tens of thousands of Black and other poor and working-class people from their home communities. Repeating the pattern of settler-colonial expansion described above, these university campuses and surrounding neighborhoods were then "secured" against outside threats and internal resistance through the development of campus police forces.

While campus police forces are less common in Canada overall, they exist on several campuses in Ontario—the University of Toronto has had campus police since 1904—and many campuses across the country have security forces that coordinate closely with local police departments. Furthermore, beyond individual campus police forces and security teams, Canadian and U.S. federal state agencies (the FBI,* RCMP,† and CSIS‡) have long monitored all levels of schooling for students, educators and activities perceived as potential threats to colonial-capitalist interests.

Dominant narratives and practices across education are intended to make racial, gendered, and class hierarchy seem natural and/ or inevitable, and to define thinking and acting against colonialism and/or capitalism as wrong. Schools are not separate from but rather are a key *part of* the carceral state. They are carceral in the presence of police officers, security guards, and federal agents; in regimes of surveillance, discipline, punishment, and coercion; in the sorting and ranking of students and control of their movement. To quote Mike Africa Jr. (author of *On a Move*, survivor of Philadelphia police bombing the MOVE house):

> The school system—there's a difference between education and schooling. Difference. The school system in America is not an educational system, it is a *schooling* system that is trying to get people to be as obedient as possible. Your job is not to be educated and be free thinkers and be critical thinkers. They don't want you to have critical thinking or critical theories; they want you to be obedient. You're okay to be critical within the parameters they lay out for you, with the borders that they put on you, with the blinders that they set on you; as long as you're within those, you're great, you're fine—A++, GPA 4.0, and all of that, whatever

---

*   Federal Bureau of Investigation
†   Royal Canadian Mounted Police
‡   Canadian Security Intelligence Service

they say. Then as you start thinking outside of those parameters, outside of those boxed walls; now you're a rebel, you're a radical, you're a nuisance, and they wanna' get you out of there.

Insurgency and Counterinsurgency

The historical and ongoing conditions described above do not mean that carceral schooling has gone uncontested, and do not mean that people do not converge in schools and do important work. Activist students, educators, staff, and community organizers have consistently claimed space for themselves and their struggles against racial capitalism *within* schools. More specifically, Black communities have always understood education and schools as central sites of our freedom struggles, and many carceral methods and policies of school discipline have specifically developed as attempts to quash assertions of Black culture, Black student autonomy, and organizing for Black liberation.

The antagonistic relationship between Black communities and carceral schools is vividly illustrated in the movement for Black Studies of the late 1960s and early 1970s. While primarily enacted in the U.S., this movement posed a serious threat to and confrontation with the proponents of colonial and carceral schooling throughout the Black diaspora. Organized Black educators, students, and communities, and their allies, fought school administrators, police forces, and governments for control of Black education, demanding profound changes to the founding assumptions and practices of schooling. In addition to promoting Black intellectualism, the Black Studies envisioned by activists was to be explicitly anti-colonial and anti-imperialist and promote radical solidarities among freedom struggles. The movement was informed by Black community-based education and organizing, and inspired by and variously connected to anti-colonial struggles in the Caribbean, Africa, and Palestine, the international anti-war movement, the German student movement, Mexican student movement, and radical coalitional movements of students and workers in places like France, Dakar, Cape Town, and Québec. The Black Panther Party at the time was highly involved in promoting and facilitating Black student organizing and demanding

Black Studies in high schools, colleges, and universities. Black activists collaborated across U.S., Canadian, and Caribbean universities and local struggles during this time, and while Canadian universities were not spared Black student resistance and direct action, they successfully refused to institutionalize Black Studies through the end of the 20th century. In the U.S., hundreds of Black Studies programs and departments were established by the early 1970s.

The vision of Black Studies was for an education contrary to that sanctioned by the state. For Black radicals, according to [*The Black Scholar*, September 1970 issue] it was to be "A Torch To Burn Down A Decadent World" of "corruption and oppression" so that freedom and justice could be nourished. It was a vision that emerged out of pre-existing "insurgent institutions" committed to popular political education that could prepare people for political struggle. As is the case now, however, disagreements about *how* Black Studies should pursue such a project were shaped by broader political differences among liberal, conservative, progressive, and radical organizers, and divided by class interests. By 1970 (and no doubt earlier) it was clear to radicals that the new Black Studies programs were at risk of being depoliticized and absorbed into existing institutions without altering the core characteristics and functions of carceral schooling. Liberal elites would help stabilize the state through aligning with private and government funders to strategically support some notions of Black Studies over others. Black Studies programs and departments struggled not only for the financial and human resources "to survive," but to meet predetermined criteria for legitimacy within academe. Such concerns, further fueled by political repression and the seduction of corporate capital, social mobility, and prestige on individuals arguably led to the capture of Black liberation struggle in education by the state; the supposed success of the movement created the conditions to turn it against itself.

To be clear, whether oriented toward reformist or revolutionary ends, any mobilization to demand "equality in the distribution of state resources" is likely to be seen by the state as a form of insurgency. Therefore, we can recognize the processes through which the radical intentions of Black Studies are pacified as those of counterinsurgency. Counterinsurgency in education—that is, action intended to demobilize activists and deter challenges to the institution—happens in many ways in addition to the use of police. For example, educational institutions form committees and task forces to examine problems like racism that continuously delay, wear out, and wait out activist students without enacting radical change; school officials appropriate the language of activists and social movements and use it in "new" policies so that it *seems* like they are committed to radical change when they are not; and schools create limited opportunities for the inclusion of Black and other individuals representing minoritized and previously excluded groups and feature these individuals in visible ways, to create the *appearance* that (white supremacist, patriarchal, elitist) institutions have changed. When individuals feel and act in loyalty to the institutions that admit or hire us, and when we are socialized into professionalism and decide that we "deserve" to live comfortable middle-class lives, we too participate in counterinsurgency. "There is no such thing as a revolutionary professor," Black Panther veteran, professor Kim Holder reminds us: "there is no such thing as a position of a professor being revolutionary. An academic institution is about maintaining the status quo."[1] This means that even when we seek to disrupt business as usual in the education system, we cannot achieve radical change from a place of professionalism and/or career-building aspirations. Academics function as counterinsurgents when they appropriate the language of grassroots activists and articulate support for abolition, Black liberation, and decolonization in their academic work, while remaining well within the boundaries of professionalism and institutional loyalty, maintaining their comfort and social-economic stability. Professionalization and careerism can turn potential insurgents into agents of the state. As the coordinator of the first Black Studies program in the U.S. predicted in 1970, "Black Studies will be revolutionary, or it will be useless if not detrimental." [*The Black Scholar*, 1970, p.2.]

Education for Liberation

The potentials of education to help us free ourselves from colonial-capitalist domination are intentionally limited and contained by schools. This does not *have to be* the case. Schools and universities do not *have to be* colonial; they are constructed that way in accordance with the nation-building projects they are meant to support. Carceral state schools teach carceral common sense. They normalize race-class social hierarchy, deference to power and authority, patriotism, competitive individualism, and compartmentalized thinking. They teach self-policing and obedience through systems of coercion, punishment, and reward. Education for liberation can and does happen when we teach and learn *against* this common sense; when we actively work to expose, resist, rethink, and transform our dominant approaches to teaching and learning. As Holder puts it [in Chapter 9, "Panther Pedagogy," *ENGAGE* (Pluto 2024)], "there is no reforming these institutions, but we can create pockets of humanistic interaction, and that needs to be our job." Education for liberation can and does happen when we choose and commit to study together, within and especially *outside* of schools; and when we learn with and from community educators and freedom fighters. We can and must reclaim education from schools.

Education for liberation is against all forms of policing. Not only against policing by police officers, but more broadly against the logics, structures, and practices of policing that shape and characterize other aspects of our lives and how we relate to one another as individuals and communities across contexts and geographies. To abolish carceral schooling is to reorient ourselves away from the multiple forms of violence that we are taught by schools and other state institutions. It is not only about the crucial work of getting cops out of K-12 schools; not only about the crucial work of resisting the ever-increasing campus police and security presence and power at universities; not only about refusing to collaborate with police or assist them in criminalizing us, our youth, and communities. It is also about refusing to become the police; refusing to adopt and enact the logics and practices of policing and carcerality that are embedded in the day-to-day functioning of educational institutions.

CHAPTER NINE

Black (Brazilian) Futurity[1]

Andréia Beatriz dos Santos, Hamilton Borges dos Santos, interview by joão costa vargas

Ancestrality

joão costa vargas (joão): Andréia and Hamilton, you mention the ways in which the dead are always present with you. Can you speak more about how the worship of ancestors informs Rise Up?*

Andréia Beatriz dos Santos (Andréia): I think this is an important aspect of the diaspora. Where I was born, in the south of the country, we learn how to worship the ancestors in a very hidden way—it was forbidden. Until recently, the prohibition was a law, there could be no African cultural manifestation without a police authorization. It's different in Bahia. Rise Up or Die! made me revisit my relationship with ancestrality.

In my father and Hamilton's first encounter, they exchanged Yoruba ancestral information via songs. My generation didn't learn those songs. My father knew them because he was an Alabê.[2] There are several African religious traditions, but they don't separate us from each other, from nature. We're a unity. Of course there's individuality, but to live we need to be in communion with nature and with each other. My existence and continuity are only possible collectively. To worship ancestrality is to recognize this interconnectedness, and to recognize who came before us, who struggled, and who didn't give up on bringing me into this world.

---

* Rise Up is an activist organization that confronts anti-Black violence in Brazil.

It's this ancestrality that we reference when we march and we say that we're ten thousand people, including the dead. Even though the people who are violently killed are not with us physically, they're part of the struggle, they're with us. We'd not exist if it were not for the relationship with those who came before us, like my father, grandfather, great grandfather, all that were in Africa. All their sacrifices made it easier for me, and for those who came after them. We say their names. We choose to reaffirm them, and establish a continuity between them and us. This worship renders impossible that we think of ourselves individually, in isolation. Collective life means that we are responsible for our own lives and the lives of others. We impact each other. African matrix religions center this worship.

vargas: Please talk more about the worship of ancestrality, not only as a spiritual aspect of Rise Up, but also as part of the practice that centers the presence of the dead.

Hamilton Borges dos Santos (Hamilton): I feel that Rise Up is the result of a spiritual determination. We didn't come up with anything new about genocide, quite the opposite. We received a legacy from the MNU [Movimento Negro Unificado (Unified Black Movement)] and we gave it our perspective, which comes from ancestrality. The first dimension of ancestrality is that we're a people. Our struggle is not related to the fact that we're exploited workers, but to the fact that, as people, we created our own humanity. We were hunted, enslaved, but we weren't victims, we didn't submit. Everywhere we are present, there is evidence of our resistance. To have instruments with which to dialogue with our ancestors is important because it gives us access to their experience, their knowledge. In my body, there's a genetic register of those experiences that allows me to look back and don't give up.

Another dimension is the exorbitant number of violent deaths over the decades, and often those deaths are mere numbers, part of our rhetoric and lament—or they're not even taken into account. You look at the history of the Black Movement in the last fifty years, there's the struggle to allow us in social elevators, universities; there's a critical debate about health, women's rights, gay rights, police brutality—but there's nothing concrete against our deaths. In Brazil, there's no accumulation of knowledge about our deaths and our lives—dignified lives. We've been immersed in death: each person we buried, we didn't talk about them based on the Coroner's Office report, or based on studies by academics. We were there, so we cite their names, we remember them as people, not as numbers: Evangivaldo, Negro Blul, Alan do Rap [were artists close to Rise Up militants who, perhaps due to their political connections, were killed by the police]. I spent more than a decade of my life burying people, now I'm gardening. But it's the same thing.

We're instruments of an ancestral Yoruba legacy, which is the devolution of the physical body to earth, which is another Orixa. When someone is killed, we have a procession with the person's body throughout the city. We politicize the dead body which until then didn't have a political value, didn't have a symbolic value, it was only yet another dead body which no one knew about.

If we were to rationalize, we'd conclude that we didn't have the conditions to undertake any of those processions and protests. We were in no condition to confront the Military Police, the state government, the Workers Party federal government, the extermination groups. Who knows what deflected the bullets away from us. The people for whom we had processions were not family members, weren't anyone we knew, but they belonged to our world, they were part of our people, so we thought it was our obligation to provide a dignified burial.

In these close encounters with death, we noticed phenomena that researchers missed. The mother who lost her son and acquired an empty gaze, she was the family's breadwinner. She ended up losing her employment as a domestic worker because she was interviewed on the TV news and her boss fired her. What did we do? Rise Up gave her basic needs, we helped with the purchase of a dignified coffin for her young son. Otherwise, the body is buried in a shallow grave, and if there's a need to exhume the body for further investigation, it's a disaster.

We knew none of this, of course—we learned because we were there. The cemeteries were not part of the Black Movement's itinerary, except to honor their militants. The militants that died usually had good burials, they came from relatively well-off backgrounds, and we'd all go there to pay our respects.

Based on our vision of the world, a Yoruba perspective that is very strong in Salvador and indeed Brazil, we developed the following perspective. Women are the primordial uterus, they create everything and they maintain the order. Exu is gold, and he stays at the crossroad waiting for the human in front of the uterus. The vagina, Ya Amapô, Mother Vagina, is an entity that's worshipped. And you have the earth, who has a pact with Obatalá, Ogun, Olugama, and Ajalané. The deities make the body, but they need the raw material, which earth lends to them, but asks that it be returned. The raw material is returned when someone dies; death is an Orixa. But death only charges what was borrowed when someone has fulfilled what they promised they'd accomplish while they were on earth, usually when someone is an elder. But death via violence, and genocide, interrupts the process. When that happens, we die two times.

In Rise Up, we debate all of this. If we come from earth and someone dies out of the natural order, you end up dying twice, and this last death is worse because, if you don't adequately return to earth—if you've been disappeared because of your politics, if you have your head cut off, if your organs are removed—you're not accepted in the realm of the dead. For a Christian, that would be an inferno.

There's no doubt that it was our capacity to dialogue with the visible and the invisible that enabled our strength and our growth, that allowed us to enter spaces we weren't supposed to enter. Obatala made my body when he blew life into it, and he sent me to earth, where I whispered in Exu's ear my goals in life. One of my original goals was to create Rise Up or Die! and create the structures that are here already. Now, imagine if I die when the cops are after me, or when I'm seventeen? My existence in the universe would be completely erased.

When we speak with young people, we help reconstitute their memory; and, in the process, they reconstitute themselves spiritually. That's when they commit to another type of life. I'm not being symbolic, or poetic. It's something in which I truly believe. I believe

111

that a lot of things happened inside the prison when I was incarcerated; police officers shot at me several times, point blank; cops going after Andréia; our home invaded by the police. We didn't have any kind of protection, nothing. All we had was our spiritual protection against a state and society that hate us.

vargas: Spiritual protection.... What happens in the moment when you know you're guided by this spiritual dimension? [For example,] the time your house was invaded by armed police officers?

Hamilton: Your intelligence is heightened and expanded. At that moment when they came for me in my house, I immediately understood what was happening. A week earlier we had been at the Nordeste de Amaralina neighborhood, where a pregnant woman had been forced into erotic positions by cops. We denounced everything, and had the press cover it.

When the cops came, I was alone at home with my son, who at the time was a toddler. I looked out of the window. I saw one of them had a machine gun. It looked homemade, probably something they seized from a drug dealer. In that moment, I called everyone I knew, and they showed up shortly thereafter. This can only be protection from another realm. I was ready to jump over into the surrounding houses with my son on my back, like a backpack—I had already spoken with him about it, as if it was a game. But many people arrived by car, by motorcycle, and the cops left. I don't know if I can explain it, but in practice, you become superhuman. I imagine a runaway enslaved person, without a map, without a weapon. Our spiritual strength shows up in those moments.

Andréia, for example, was nicknamed pejoratively "super Black woman" (*super negona*) when the police brutalized a young person during a show in Barra. When I protested, they arrested me. Undeterred, Andréia confronted the police officers, and hit a police officer's baton with her sandal. She then hit the cops, including a woman officer, whom she slapped and scratched. That called the attention of a lot of people. Now, if there was no reaction, if Andréia didn't confront them, who knows where they would have taken me, and what they would have done. Andréia did not accept the silence, and she reacted. She became the super Black woman.

vargas: So, this spiritual protection is the consciousness that—in the crucial moment—you are being protected?

Hamilton: Your ancestors accompany you; for that to happen, you have to be attuned to them. And in Rise Up we have this connection with the dead, we remember the impoverished Black people, we remember their cries. These people stay with us, they support us. I've had brothers from my Candomblé house tell me to stop talking about the dead, "they'll bring bad things for you." I tell them they don't bring bad things to me—I'm taking care of their families. I'm keeping their memories alive.

I have a dream project of writing a book with the faces and the histories of each one of the people we accompanied, including the number of their burial site, so that they stay alive for the centuries ahead of us, and then they can return to earth and fulfill their life proposals. It's very difficult for Black people to fulfill our proposals. And for me, it's all about fulfilling our proposals.

vargas: When we take into account the pervasiveness of violent death of Black people you both narrate, we have to emphatically reject the myth that Brazil, differently than the U.S., doesn't have a history and present marked by lynching. Lynching of Black people is pervasive in Brazil. I'm hearing your dream project as a description of a book based on your archives of lynchings.

Hamilton: I remember the death of Pit, who was one of the local criminal faction's founders. The police were after him, and then they kill him following a chase. We sent a document to the federal Human Rights office showing he was lynched. Pit was one of eight similar deaths, but his was more cruel; because, following the chase and gunfire exchange, he turns himself in. His body shows up with the arms broken and a shot in the back of the head. But the police claim he was killed during the gunfire exchange. How can you say he was killed while he was shooting when his arms are broken and he's shot in the back of the head? There was no investigation.

Pressured by our protests and work behind the scenes, the local police became somewhat more accountable in 2007, 2008. But then a federal police chief wrote in a major newspaper that the Bahia police are soft. The next day, Evangivaldo was killed with nine shots. We know he was no saint, he was a drug dealer, he was cruel, he beat up people. Still, we insist the state cannot be vengeful, it needs to follow the rule of law. That's why we don't have a democracy. While they dragged the bodies, the police sang their anthem, in front of the mothers. The mothers of state victims are with us and like us because they see how committed we are.

We invented the general theory of failure because we're not successful at anything. We didn't succeed in suing any of the police officers, we didn't change the police violent approach; rather the opposite, the police received more weapons, and people became more intimidated. We failed at everything. Maybe Andréia disagrees. I think we failed in our proposal of bringing freedom to our people. We're not going to be successful as long as we're asking for certain public policy and as long as we're expecting conscientious and caring institutions.

We're only going to be successful when the people who are harmed organize themselves. But organizations that are historically Black, or have a lot of Black people in them, don't want to get involved: soccer, Church, Candomblé, and even the drug traffickers, who are the greatest providers of resources in our communities (cooking gas, schools, daycare centers, telephone, internet, etc.) We have to deal with all of that, it's not just the state in its raw force. We have to deal with our own people's cynicism. We are different because we're not giving up.

One of the mothers who, a few years ago, witnessed her son dragged and killed by the police, she called us about two weeks ago. She wanted to speak with Andréia. She didn't call asking us to organize a meeting in the neighborhood; she didn't call because we were able to get some compensation from the state for her son's death; she called because she likes us. It's difficult because people expect that we do everything. We tell them they need to get involved... [and] to be in charge. Then there's another death, and three hundred people show up here, and there's an expectation that we'll do all the organization and mobilization.

vargas: In the inaugural ceremony yesterday, when Lula took office, there was a symbolically strong scene in which Black women, Black children, and people with disabilities were represented.[3] From the perspective of Rise Up or Die! how did you make sense of that moment?

Hamilton: Yesterday, after watching the entire event, I wrote an essay in which I say "hopelessness is a zeal." I wrote this because there's so much hope, happiness, euphoria for things that, for us, are merely symbolic. I'm saying this because we've been here before. It's the third time we're in this symbolism. We don't live in the symbolic world. We live in the real concrete world.

I'll give you an example. I don't drink alcohol, I stay sober. I don't use anything that alters the reality. In such a harsh world, it's hard to live like this. I think the energy during Lula's inauguration was beautiful, it was good. But we know there's the day after. When the carnival is over, we're left with reality. Many Rise Up people don't believe in any of this symbology. But Black people in general, we're too naive. Yet those who supposedly represent us in such spaces of power, they're not naive. They have a very well-defined project of power; they put their family members in those institutions, which will guarantee that they have much better prospects than most Black people: they will be able to get formal education, they'll have employment, they'll be financially stable.

But our concern is with the majority of our people. It remains with nothing. For us, as Andréia said, public policy is like a placebo. It has a psychological effect on us. You may have more buying power, you buy nice clothes, TV, refrigerator, but you don't buy land, you don't buy a house, you don't have financial investments, you don't leave a financial inheritance. I voted for Lula in 1989. This current moment is beautiful theater. But it doesn't reflect reality. Andréia mentioned Snoop Doggy Dog and compared Pele with Muhammad Ali. But it's a bad comparison. Ali had a commitment toward his people. I've heard comparisons between Lula and Nelson Mandela. Lula is a white man.

We Black people need to stop adoring white people. You look at his ministries, he put Black people in symbolic posts devoid of power. What will a Human Rights minister do? For that position, Lula appointed a Black man, Sílvio Almeida. What is Almeida going to do when I come to his office and say that I want to denounce Rui Costa, who is the current federal minister of Institutional Relations and was the governor of the state of Bahia, for genocide against Black people? Almeida may even find time to see me, and he may try to do something, but we know nothing will happen.

Then there's the ministry of the Promotion of Racial Equality. The very notion of equality is harmful. The debate is rooted in an old discussion about whether Black people are human, and between two white men lawyers in particular, Rui Barbosa and Clovis Bevilaqua in the early 1900s.[4] And we are still debating equality. There's an elder MNU activist who used to say "Black people want equality with whites, but whites don't want to be equal to Black people." Even the Landless Movement send out a press release saying that social movements now need to be the government's base, and strengthen it. For me, this makes no sense. That's why I feel isolated. In this conjuncture, there's no more space for us. We're going to have to forge our own space. We have to elaborate a new strategy for our struggle. We can't struggle like we did in 2005. We lived the pandemic apocalypse. We need to start over; we need a new birth.

We have a political obligation to mobilize people and communities, we need to develop oppositional thinking, and create spaces of joy, happiness, and abundance. Only then we'll be able to confront state and society. And when we do so, we'll have to confront the Black people who are the watchdogs. They don't appear in photos, but they're doing a lot of work behind the scenes. Some of them are truly excellent people, I respect them.

White people dominate those spaces of power. Lula's tactic was to throw himself toward the center right, that's why he got Alckmin as his vice president. The government's goal is to strengthen the market economy and guarantee minimum survival conditions for the people. But we don't expect land reform, we don't expect de-carceration, we don't expect a deep debate about those topics, especially about public security.

vargas: Given the strong symbology and magnetism of the Workers Party, how do you approach the younger people, how do talk about the weaknesses of the government program regarding Black people?

Hamilton: Some people think Rise Up doesn't have concrete proposals, and that we only complain and lament. This also happens regarding our writing. I write literary fiction, and I talk about genocide, hunger, and hopelessness. When I'm among writers, at an event for example, I often hear, as a critique against my writing, "we need to talk about middle-class Black people." It's the same critique regarding our analysis. They say we only talk about terror, failure, and we don't present anything new. It reminds me of Malcolm X and how he was ostracized from the mainstream Civil Rights Movement that dialogued with a white agenda. But Malcolm emphasized the need to have our own agenda, to have our own thought.

We try to show that our analysis and our literature come from the most wretched places, like prisons, impoverished and violent areas. But most people want to enjoy life, have a beer. It's like they're anaesthetized. There's no political discussion—politics has been destroyed, it has become synonymous with elections, and the monetary and power transactions that happen before, during, and after them.

We keep trying. We started a communitarian garden. We tell folks that they need to reject the food that's sold in the local supermarket, which is owned by whites who don't live here and who are just draining our resources away from our area. The food from that supermarket is making people sick: we get diabetes, high [blood] pressure. We live in a food desert. The food that's available is unhealthy and is not inspected by the consumer protection service. When we bring this up, no one is interested in talking about it. There are no alternative perspectives. For a long time, we were a source of alternative thought here in Salvador, and that's because we talked about death, which is the most sensitive topic. We were in the cemeteries, we were in the Coroner's Office, we were in front of the police station. In all these places, we flirted with death. We were dealing with profound pain in the families of victims of police brutality. We hated the police and said so. We created a narrative for those experiences, a Black radical perspective, that had nothing to do with the narrative of Human Rights, which whites dominate.

We told whites that we accept their solidarity, but we also told them that they'd have no voice in our marches, rallies, and events. We organized a lot of local, state, and national events, as we mentioned earlier. In all of them, we collectively came up with alternative models of safety, health, Black politics, society, and the state. White folks were not prepared for this. Frankly, Black people weren't either.

All this was very tiring and hurtful. I can't do it any more: I can't deal with that pain, that tiredness, with having to crash into official meetings, go to Military Police stations. I can't deal with being persecuted and vilified by white and Black people. I don't have the energy anymore.

Now we're focusing on transforming our school into a great political school, a place where political thought will be debated and reverberate. It will also strengthen political practice in communities. Rise Up is turning eighteen this year, and along this time we forged our political perspective: we've been debating racism, death, and genocide, the international character of the struggle, quilombismo. Today we're convinced the perspective on anti-blackness is fundamental. With revolutionary patience, we'll bring in and develop ties with people from all over Brazil as well as folks from South Africa, Europe, the U.S., and various parts of the Black Americas.

More immediately, we want to bring together people who think differently than us. Like bringing together the Crips and Bloods. We want to sit around a table and reflect together. It wouldn't be the left or the right, it'd be us. It would be like an advanced nucleus of the struggle. We want to call for a great National Action Program, a political project for the country. There is no possibility for changing this country except via political action—it won't be via political parties or digital influence. Many social movements said they don't have a project for the country other than electing Lula. That is not our project.

vargas: You're thinking of a broad political front?

Hamilton: Exactly. There are folks in the south of Bahia already working the land; there's the hip hop people. Our obstacle is the distrust of us, but we can get over it.

vargas: Andréia, what is Rise Up's analysis of this moment when Lula was inaugurated yesterday, when Pelé, who recently passed,[5] is now someone who, according to press commentators, had or inspired a critical analysis of Brazil's race relations, despite being timid, at best, during his entire life around such issues.[6] It seems that we're going through a rapid revision of our recent history.

Andréia: It's important to point out that Black people like Pelé, Anielle Franco, Sílvio Almeida, they're not a problem for us. They provide a shield for our greatest problem, which is white supremacy. We obviously don't want to disregard the experience of a Black woman like Franco. Rather, we want to emphasize that, in order to confront racism—to which the Lula administration claims it is committed—the process should have been different. Whose voice is being heard, and who's occupying high-level posts in the Ministry of Women, Family and Human Rights and the Ministry of Racial Equality? It feels like we've been through this before. Despite the Ministry of Racial Equality's recognition that there's an extermination of young Black people in course, genocide continues. I don't think filling posts with Black people will make any difference. But we may be surprised. Maybe people in those offices may facilitate, or may be sensitive to various denunciations of police brutality and lethality, the continued disappearance of young Black people, and how Black communities are multiply impacted by these and other processes that lead to preventable death of Black people. Particularly the denunciations that originate in international organizations.

In relation to Pelé's death, as in the passing of other Black icons, his racial belonging was rendered invisible during their lifetime, or at least diluted. It happens to all of us. Pelé was treated like a king, which required that his African heritage and background be silenced, including the struggles that his father and mother, who were quite humble, went through in the interior of the Minas Gerais state, where the legacies of agricultural slavery and corrupt and violent politics certainly affected them.

As a dark-skinned person like him, my problem is not with Pelé, it's with white supremacy. It's always quite easy to blame a Black person for what they didn't do. He could have been more outspoken about racial issues, but then perhaps he wouldn't be treated and benefited like a king. Same thing with Anielle, I don't want to criticize her. But we know there were other names of Black people with a longer political trajectory—including some who are part of the Workers Party base—who are qualified and would try to radicalize the ministry. The work of white supremacy is extensive.

The same deradicalization happened in the state of Bahia. In preparation for the 2020 mayoral election, the Workers Party discussed potential candidates. Due to the historical moment, Salvador being the largest Black city outside the African continent, there was a sense that a Black woman should be the candidate. But instead of supporting Black women who had a trajectory in social movements, big political bosses, white men like Rui Costa and the senator Jacques Wagner, supported Denice Santiago Santos do Rosario, a Black Military Police Major who is also a psychologist. It seems to me that Anielle Franco and Silvio Almeida's presence is similar insofar as it is part of a white supremacist project that allows certain Black people to have some form of power.

vargas: Hamilton mentioned that he's exhausted, and that he can't continue doing the same types of interventions he's been doing for decades. Do you feel the same way?

Andréia: From a woman's perspective, it's different. My mother, aunts, and sisters taught me to see the world in a particular manner. My relationship with Rise Up is the same as my relationship with my teenager Black son. At the end of each day, I'm exhausted. I look at what I had to endure, and I look at what needs to be done tomorrow.

I feel the same way as Hamilton about Rise Up in terms of the tiredness. But our exhaustion gives us perspective. It's a moment when we realize we can't go on like we did until now. It's necessary to bring in new people and build collectively, forging new paths.

I remember my mother when she looked at the empty pantry, two weeks into the month, and wondered how we'd make the next two weeks. It would have to be just rice and beans until the next month when my father's salary came in. I learned from her. Collectively, we evoke this kind of knowledge, and we figure it out. I remember my mother's tired gaze; but she persisted. It's part of me now, and we'll find a way.

Rise Up turns eighteen in 2023, and we're happy not because we have a lot, but because we feel like we've done enough to explore new paths, and harvest what we planted along the way. We're happy because, while striving for autonomy, we've been able to reorient ourselves. We can't go on like we did in the last eighteen years, which were of utmost importance. We spent many sleepless nights, I did many night shifts at work, not knowing how we'd pay for the school's rent, how we'd offer children a snack, and so many other daily demands that were put on us with the expectation that we'd resolve things immediately.

Now we're looking at this differently, recognizing we need to strengthen ourselves. Today we can't carry as many rocks as we did, but those rocks have been placed, the corner stone is in place. We need to continue building.

We've done so much that we never had time to celebrate some of our achievements; we didn't realize how many seeds we planted. With very limited resources, we put in a great investment of our time, and we had support from many people. We can't really say we are tired. We have a continued commitment with so many people. Our lives continue to be devalued. The former Bahia governor, now a Lula administration minister, continues to belittle the twelve young people who were killed in Cabula.* The victims' mothers are discouraged. Our role is to continue the struggle, not with false hope, but with a commitment to collectively build our future. With each name we're going to remember on February 6, 2023, on the

---

* See "Brazil: Twelve people killed by military police," Amnesty International, February 16, 2015.

eighth anniversary the Cabula massacre, we're also evoking hope of a better collective future. Otherwise, the struggle is meaningless.

vargas: Can you talk about your vision of the future?

Andréia: I think we need to rescue the power that Black women have, and build collectively. When we look at the mothers who lost their children to police brutality, despite all the sadness, they try to carry on with their daily lives. They help neighbors, they're active, they search for a light in their lives. It's very inspiring in the sense that we have to project a future and rescue this energy that we call the Vital Command, which is the force that allows us to continue on, and continue building.

In their families, while women keep things moving, everyone's alright. They do the shopping, they do the planning, the cleaning, they come to meetings—they bake a cake and make coffee to bring to the meeting, they recognize everyone's in the struggle and we need to eat. Today I can see more clearly how the collective reconstruction takes place, and the central place women have in it. In our school, we have a Formation Center, and it's a happy place, bright, beautiful. On the walls we have representations of our own history. We can't forget it; we can't think that we're restarting from scratch. We have the conditions from which to consolidate all the communitarian work that we've accomplished, and I think this is our vision of the future.

Yesterday, Sunday, we ran into Wagner, who was one of the first students at the Winnie Mandela school. Today he's seventeen or eighteen. It struck us how vulnerable Wagner is, unfortunately. All we wanted was to protect him from so many forms of harm and danger. When we met him and his family, and we saw his smile, it brought home that the work is not done, but rather, that we have to press on. There's no end to the work. We have to consolidate this space as ours, where dark-skinned Black people are protected and are building collectively. We're building a legacy not only for the future, but also for the present everyday life. We're going to plant this seed in other communities. We're dealing with a continuous, gigantic, and complex problem, and we have to confront it, there's no other way. This is what is going to nourish us.

vargas: The concept of the Vital Command indicates both the accumulation of political knowledge, and how Black women have always found ways to guarantee the community survival and therefore that of future generations. Your encounter with Wagner suggests an encounter with the future, and what needs to be done. It helped me grasp the importance of the Vital Command, and how it is rooted in ancestral knowledge women carry with them. It's quite a contrast to the perspective of men. Am I hearing some optimism here?

Andréia: I'm going to search for "optimism" in the dictionary because sometimes I think there are certain words that lose their meaning. I think what we have is pragmatism with relation to what's in front of us, not so much optimism. I was born in the midst of all this. I'm the heir of people who decided they'd insist on organizing themselves so that I could be where I am today, with a level of sanity and being able to make choices. I could make choices. I've been making choices in my fifty years of life, thanks to the choices my parents made, and their parents before, and so on.

The pragmatism that I mentioned is the same that I heard in the conversations between the women in my family. In family gatherings, when women were by ourselves, we discussed all kinds of matters and planned ahead. Often, we had to come up with solutions to different types of problems, there was no other way. I carry that pragmatism, and I think that, as I mature, I'm learning to value it even more. We continue to dream—and this is also fundamental—but when we wake up from a dream and we have its memory, we have to be pragmatic as to how we implement the dream.

vargas: I'm hearing you describe a type of insistent pragmatism, one that doesn't give up even when faced with overwhelming circumstances.

Andréia: When mothers bring their newborns to protest in front of the Military Police or the Ministry of Public Security, that's the pragmatism I'm talking about. It's what needs to be done. I worked through many nights to generate much needed resources for Rise Up; then slept for three hours and went to an organizing activity in the prison. In the way that I understand my role in the collective, that's what needed to be done. When we risk ourselves in the confrontations with the police, it's the result of the collective struggle pragmatism that recognizes the necessity of opposition, resistance, and survival; it also insists in carrying forward our own project. This makes us believe in the possibility of doing something, a belief nourished in the practice. I don't think we can implement our vision in any space; what we proposed ourselves to do is only possible in certain spaces, and in those spaces, we can protect and defend what we've done.

vargas: It seems that the Vital Command, based on Black women's knowledge, is also a collective survival engineering: they know what needs to be done, and if they don't, they'll invent something.

Andréia: Exactly. Those who stayed in Rise Up know we must restructure ourselves, and we'll find a way. There are so many anonymous Black women who guaranteed the survival of their family without any kind of support. They constructed some of their knowledge in the practice, and we also inherited knowledge from our elders.

My mother certainly didn't have a manual on how to raise four Black kids, and she had no instructions on how to make it possible that all four had choices and flourished. She learned in the process, relying on family, neighbors, friends. And simple things that she passed on to us: "if you eat everything at lunch, there's not going to be dinner." Simple things. "Put more water in the beans; divide up the food." These are things that my mother still says. The process is quite beautiful.

vargas: There's no graspable manual, but maybe it's available at some level. I imagine your manual is similar to your mother's, which was similar to her parents'. And then it gets expanded and adapted?

Andréia: Certainly, this vital force is passed on from generation to generation. Various codes and instructions are transmitted that way, which we grasp only with time. Some of the things my mother said, only now I get it: when I think about groceries for the month, my son's school supplies, and when we had to come up with snacks for twenty-seven kids at the school.

At the Winnie Mandela school, how were we going to build a routine, a curriculum? We had no help from education specialists. Based on the children we knew, including my own, we came up with a routine: when students arrived, they started with the homework; then there's a collective moment and a time to read in group. Then we taught them how to wash their hands, brush their teeth—there was a session on personal hygiene.

As we got cohorts with older kids, we also talked about sexual development, including body changes in puberty—at that point we got help from women who had expertise in those topics. As we developed our school, some of the many codes that were passed to us began to make sense and were applied; we drew from the manual, as it were. We carry many of the codes and the manual in us, I agree with you.

We talked about the letters my father wrote. That's how I look into the future—as he looked, as my mother looked: projecting, constructing. When we look at the manifestos that we wrote for each of the annual marches, we talk about what we accomplished, but we also talk about what we want to do. So, they are letters for the future, they're manifestos of our continuity.[7]

vargas: Every time I've been at the school, I felt like I was in a spaceship, and now I see why. It has to do with this vision of the future, in this insistent engineering that refuses to stop.

Andréia: It's good to hear that. There's the nagging thought that maybe we're not doing enough, or not doing it right. We revisit

history, we reflect on it, and we retell our own history—that nourishes us. That's why it's important to write about what we have
accomplished; it brings renewed energy. We've done so much that
often we forget about it. It gets lost.

vargas: Hamilton, what is your dream, what does it look like?

Hamilton: I have a dream in three dimensions: short term, medium
term, long term. The latter two dimensions are in my latest book. In
the short term, it's the remodeling of the Rise Up headquarters to
make it a dignified space, a beautiful and inviting space where we
debate and exchange knowledge, we experiment artistically and sci-
entifically. We'll spread the ideas from the Winnie Mandela school.

In 2004, 2005, during our Provocation Wednesdays, we were
already thinking about this Pan-Africanist school. At this point, I
don't think it's as much Africanist as it is quilombista, from a radical
experience of Africans in Brazil, which we continue to develop.

Medium term, we have to expand our experience of struggle to
new territories, we're calling it the New Zumbi Quilombos (Os
Novos Quilombos de Zumbi, from a Caetano Veloso song.) This
project involves the fields of health, law, literature, arts, agriculture.
We're going to bring books, ideas, debates to the communities that
today are completely emptied of dignity.

At eighteen, Rise Up or Die! has reached its adulthood. We've
reached a point at which when there's a police homicide of a Black
person, there's widespread lamentation. The press, the academics,
folks in the streets, they talk about it but there's no movement. It's as
if an outer space alien landed, killed the person, and left: there's no
cause, there's no one responsible for the death.

We're desperate and hopeless. We want to go to those places that
are the most challenged and say that there are possibilities for us
to build communities in which we can breathe, we can think inde-
pendently, and we can dream. To dream is an indispensable tool.
The African deities, all of them, they dream. When we dream, we
also realize the dream. As things stand, I don't see any possibility
for Black people in one hundred years. As Fred Aganju says, worse
days will come, and they're already here. In Salvador, Porto Alegre,

São Paulo, there's already water shortage, and reservoirs are at their limit.

vargas: I'm hearing that the quilombo you dream of is mostly, if not entirely, composed of dark-skinned Black people, who would be the initiative's political and theoretical agents, is that correct?

Hamilton: in my book of fiction, *Bantu Machine*, dark-skinned Black people can be killed at any time, and there are no consequences because they don't have any value in the Enclosed City. They're only valued in the quilombo, that's why they're constantly fleeing the city. Nonblack people don't have a say in this project. If they're allies, and they have resources, they should contribute.

The lighter-skinned people have associations with spheres of power, and live a more tranquil life; they try to promote dialogue between whites and Black people, and they tell Black people that, if you don't revolt, the system is good and won't kill you. So, the book is for Black people. If you're able to build a quilombo from a quilombista perspective, the strategies will be quilombista, and the affect and love will be quilombista too.

Light-skinned Black people need to define themselves. They need to say what they want, and what side they're on. Sometimes I look at light-skinned people's social media, and I only see them with white people. They're not in places where there's a Black majority, they don't want that. I think no one wants to be with us. Maybe because we're too loud, too angry.

I was brought up in the Black Movement of the 1970s. In its bylaws, there was something that caught my attention, and today I wonder about it. It said "Black is the person who has traits that are typical of the race." It was a very broad definition, but I think it included mixed-race Black people like my great grandmother, who was considered *sarará* [mixed]. I don't think the definition included people like Antonio Carlos Magalhães Neto, a politician who claims to be "mixed."[8]

Aílton Krenak, an Indigenous intellectual, said that in the 1990s, in the face of genocide, it was decided that the vital strategy of survival for Indigenous people was to marry and have as many children as possible. It's the same for us, to continue existing and dreaming, we need to have Black children.

According to the Brazilian Census, dark Black people like me are only 7% of the population. We're not the majority, like the Black Movement claims. We are unmistakably Black. Ask Andréia if she has any doubt. But there are light-skinned people who say "I discovered myself Black in college;" or "I discovered myself Black when I came to Salvador." Dark-skinned people are stopped in the streets, the police look at us differently. To this day, when I'm surrounded by white people, I feel out of place.

In 2020, there were many live virtual events on Black literature. But there were no Black people. Literary scholar Jovina Souza and Andréia called my attention to it. We feel this on our skin. Light-skin privilege is everywhere, including in the prisons, where the leadership also tends to be lighter-skinned.

I'm not saying that a light-skinned Black person doesn't suffer. Yet racism's sequelae impact dark-skinned people more directly. You look at who's incarcerated, and you'll see they are mostly dark-skinned. On the other hand, in academia, most Black people are light-skinned. And when I'm near them, they clutch their belongings. It's very draining. I catch myself policing myself, and I'm concerned about everyone around me. I don't know if there are people who can live at peace with that, but I can't.

Recently, I went to a clinic for a consultation, and the doctor kept the door open the entire time. She only opened the door when I was there. It's very hard for us. Doctors don't touch us. And some of them say they're Black—at least at the university, where they claim racial quotas by invoking a parent or grandparent who is Black. I feel that light-skinned folks are not willing to engage in any kind of radical struggle, and that's because they have a lot to lose. In Curuzu, the neighborhood where I grew up, is the place where there's more Black people in Salvador. There, the lighter-skinned people have the larger houses; the police don't bother them.

vargas: Andréia, you mentioned that you dream, and that when you wake up and remember the dream, pragmatically you have to figure out how to implement it. What do you dream of?

Andréia: We dream a lot. The school was a dream. The idea of having our own building was a dream, but there were other demands and that was put on the backburner. In order to accomplish all those things, we have to dream first, and without the dream there would be no pragmatic strategy. Even after we started the school, we didn't know where the rent for the second month was going to come from. We bought a bunch of things on credit, and our credit card was done. We dream about having a communitarian organization buzzing with Black people.

I imagine that inside the Palmares quilombo everything was not wonderful all the time; the same during the uprisings. Things are complex, and so is our presence in the world. The people who came before me, my blood ancestors, they must have suffered immeasurably for me to get here.

We're also going to go through many trials. That's why it's so critical to dream. We dream with our feet on the ground—we must continue to build, but we have to be realistic, and even expect internal betrayals. We have to anticipate having the rug taken from under our feet by those who were supporting us.

We continue to seek articulations with folks who study, who are scholars, but they seem to distance themselves from the reality of the carceral system, the reality of Black women, of impoverished people, who are often in the same areas where we live. In our own neighborhood we have several unhoused people, people going through food insecurity. Since the turn of the year, the area has been under siege. There's a dispute between the police and drug dealers. When I visit certain areas around here, to offer medical consultation—areas you can't drive to—I give a three-day notice so that everyone knows it's me that's coming, and I'm not mistaken for someone else.

What we dream of, what we visualize, is to continue going to those places we've been going to in the last eighteen years, and continue building. Those places continue to not have basic sanitation, they flood when it rains. People go hungry. In truth, this is what nourishes us.

My main dream, which is becoming more crystalized as we talk, is to have a group of Black women who are empowered and able to produce our own history, starting with their families, their communities. It would be a multitude of Black women, organized, conscious. It would be an army of Black women. The image that comes to mind is that of a woman with a child in one arm, and a rifle in the other. But at other times, it will be food instead of the rifle; a book; a blanket. When we organize our events, we see this potential that is stored in Black women's strength that sustain their families and communities.

That's the image I have for our quilombo. People producing their own food, in a clean place, unpolluted, worshiping orixas and ancestrality—this soothes my heart, and excites me. But it requires that we go plant our feet in the mud, jump over open sewage, to provide food for those in need. All the while maintaining the communitarian project in which we discuss possible futures.

We need to resignify the model of the state which we have internalized, which only benefits white people. We need to cut ourselves from those concepts of governmentality. There's more than 70 million people who go through moderate food insecurity.[9] [Vin`icius Lisboa, "Food Insecurity Affects 70mi Brazilians UN Report Shows," *agenciaBrasil*, July 15, 2023.]

This is a long-term project, and it involves bringing more people on board. We meet people in the street who say "I want to visit the school. I was in jail. When I was away from you, I could see what you were doing and what you were saying. I now understand, and I know how I can help. I have one day in the week."

So, we're building. The problem is complex, and its roots are profound. Unlike white people, we can't put numbers to our small victories. We're going to bring more people out of the mud. It's a possible reality, and Black women provide examples. They're looking ahead with their children. We know of a family with five women, no adult men. Some of their companions died, others were incarcerated, or became drug addicts. The women stayed with the kids. They do domestic work, they hustle, and in between their daily activities they take the kids to school; they organize second-hand clothes sales in their home, and we help them with basic foods. It's women like them that make up the army I dream of.

CHAPTER TEN

When Opportunity Knocks ... by Gallery of the Streets

Gallery of the Streets (kai barrow, Jazz Franklin, Kara Lynch)

The prisoners of Miserabilism need a win. The rise of a new kkkourt has released a campaign of terror marked by military training grounds, mandatory work kkkamps, and neighborhood soldiers of fortune. Organizing (even if unsuccessful) has become a level 10 crime, punishable by death. Surveillance, snitches, and sell outs, control the MARVELOUS from within the interior. A TRICKSTER must devise a winning strategy.

This hybrid visual essay, an excerpt from our larger work, *[b]REACH: adventures in heterotopia*, a Black surrealist opera, is part organizer's toolkit, part speculative fiction, part study guide.

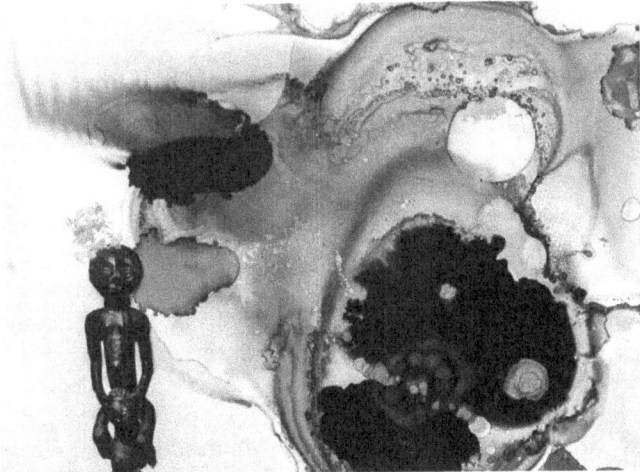

The visual libretto reads as an abolitionist code, a collage of maps, charts, constellations, historical anecdotes, script excerpts, reference materials, and abstractions for will-be fugitives to consider when outwitting the nitwits, narcissists, neanderthals, neocons, and neo-colonialists.

Act One: The Book Of Air
It's a question of urgency: How will we communicate when EMPIRE cuts the cord?

Episode 1: When opportunity knocks …

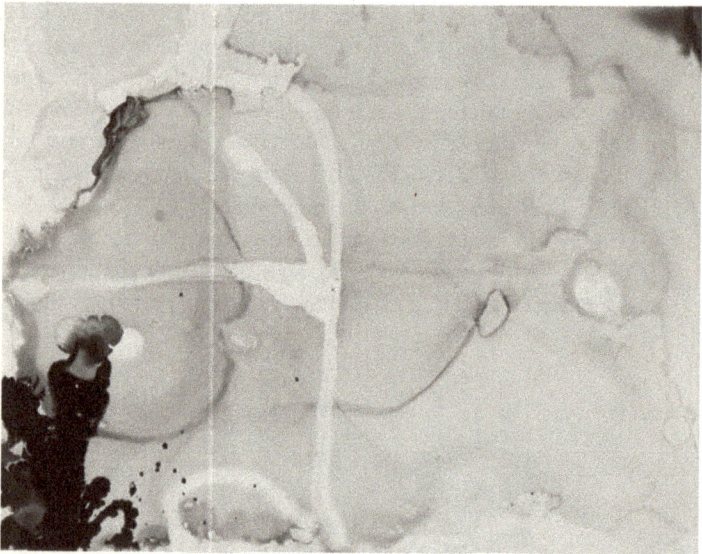

Trapped on a bus to nowhere (good), the ten members of the MARVELOUS, aka, the Prisoners from Cellblock #25, sat two to a row, ankle-cuffed to one another and surrounded by EMPIRE's goons. Looking and listening for opportunities to escape, they read the space, spotted the signs, and spoke to one another in the language of the oppressed: eye-rolls, head nods and lip curls. The two MAGAts transporting them to the next state of Miserabilism sat in the front, singing along to the hits on Empire Radio and reading aloud to the prisoners from the "NO, NOT, & DON'T HANDBOOK".

[MAGAt's duet, 'NO, NOT, & DON'T']

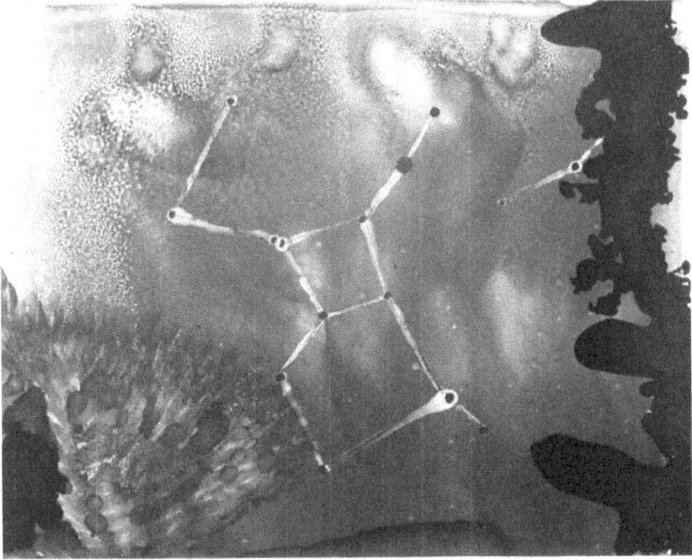

When the *Empire Anthem*, the latest chart topper, came across the airwaves, the MAGAts lost it. They saluted their flag, punched the air, howled the hook, and taunted the prisoners, pointing to the pages of rules covering every surface of the bus. As the crescendo built, the MAGAts threw their heads back in wild abandon, violently shaking their heads and shoulders and promptly crashed the bus into a … Wormhole? Pot hole? Texas? Florida?

[Sounds of Static, 'Ten Minutes of Static'[1]]

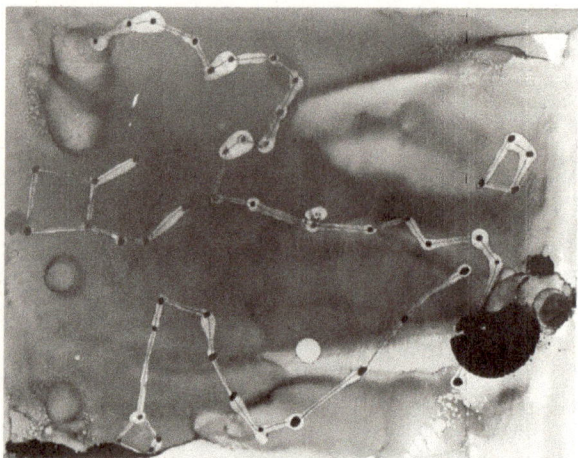

As the MAGAts got out of the bus to check the damage, cuss the prisoners (just because), and call for help, a voice pierced through the static on the radio. DJ TRICKSTER directed the prisoners, who sat motionless, to take action.

[Amina Claudine Myers, 'Steal Away/Athan (Call to Prayer)/Fatiha (Sura Prayer)'[2]]

Episode 2: Escape ...

After commandeering the bus and finding a hiding place, the Prisoners from Cellblock #25, now fugitives, could not believe their luck. With DJ TRICKSTER bumping the marronage playlist, they found allies in the shadows who cut their chains, provided care and community, and helped them repurpose the bus. They knew the MAGAts were on the hunt and had to work quickly to make a plan.

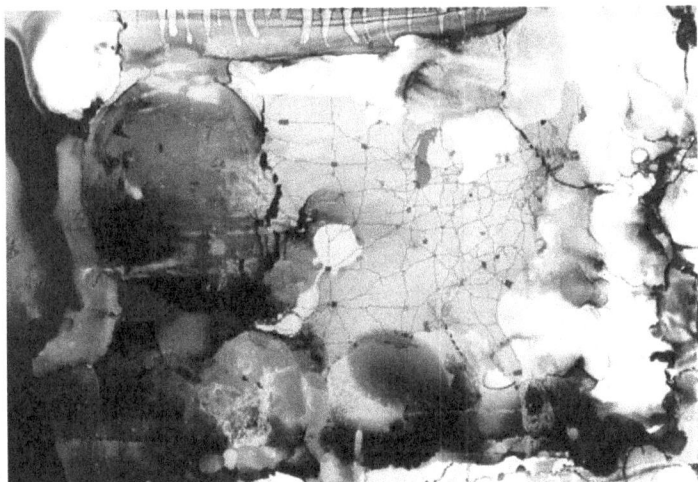

Episode 3: Fugitive cartographies ...

The fugitives debated safe(r) routes, predicted worst- and better-case scenarios, and made maps out of scraps, scribblings, symbols, and nonsense. Realizing that the fascists had built a police state to fence in the MARVELOUS and control their movements, the fugitives had no other options. The time had come to smash the state.

[Jayne Cortez and the Firespitters, 'There It Is']³

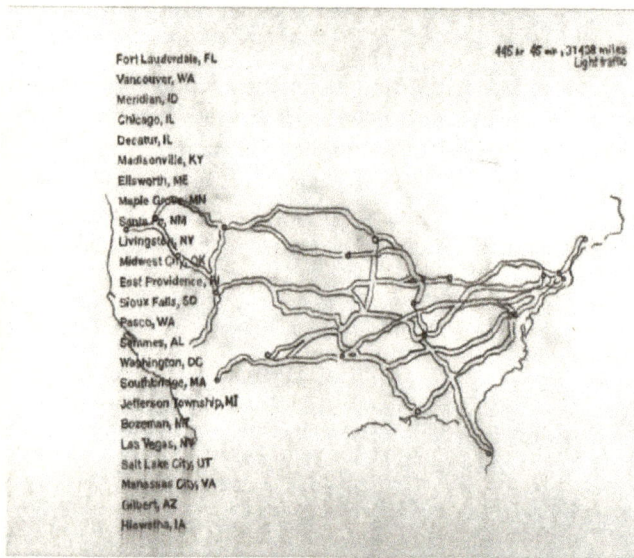

Fort Lauderdale, FL
Vancouver, WA
Meridian, ID
Chicago, IL
Decatur, IL
Madisonville, KY
Ellsworth, ME
Maple Grove, MN
Santa Fe, NM
Livingston, NY
Midwest City, OK
East Providence, RI
Sioux Falls, SD
Pasco, WA
Satsuma, AL
Washington, DC
Southbridge, MA
Jefferson Township, MI
Bozeman, MT
Las Vegas, NV
Salt Lake City, UT
Manassas City, VA
Gilbert, AZ
Hiawatha, IA

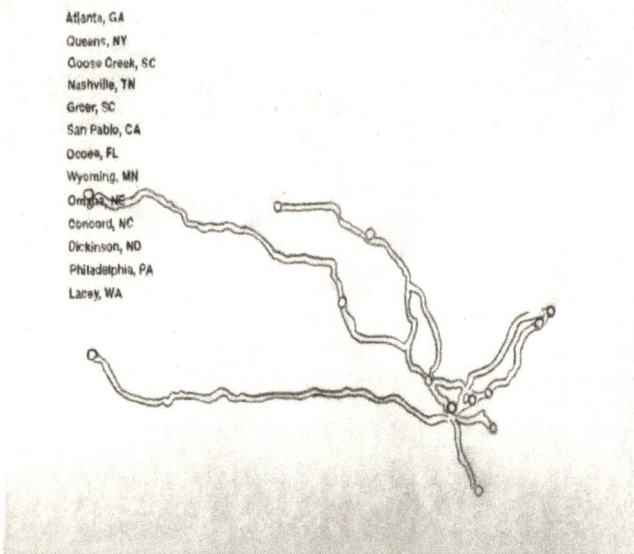

Atlanta, GA
Queens, NY
Goose Creek, SC
Nashville, TN
Greer, SC
San Pablo, CA
Ocoee, FL
Wyoming, MN
Omaha, NE
Concord, NC
Dickinson, ND
Philadelphia, PA
Lacey, WA

Determined to bring down EMPIRE, they named themselves RADIO OUTLAW as a shout-out to DJ TRICKSTER, and vowed to alert the MARVELOUS of the dangers that lay ahead. If they could entice others to create fugitive spaces and resistance pods, there might be a chance to save the world from the expanding carceral state.

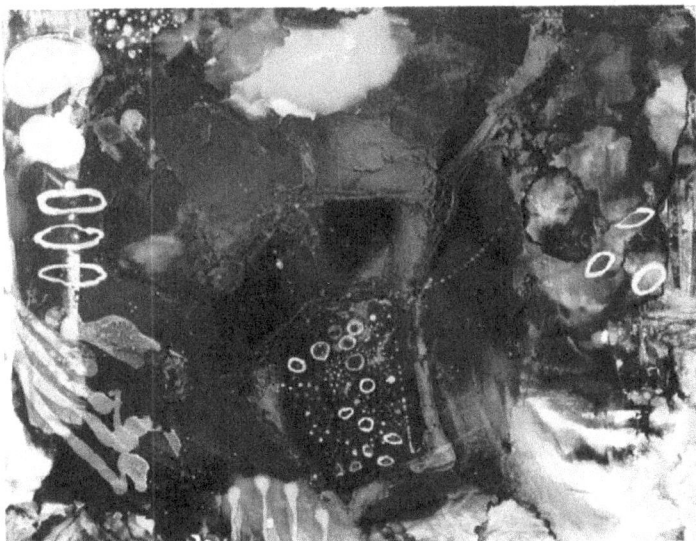

Episode 4: How to set up a mobile autonomous communication unit from recycled, upcycled, found objects and donated equipment ...

[Max Roach and Abbey Lincoln, 'Triptych: Prayer/Protest/Peace (Remastered)'][4]

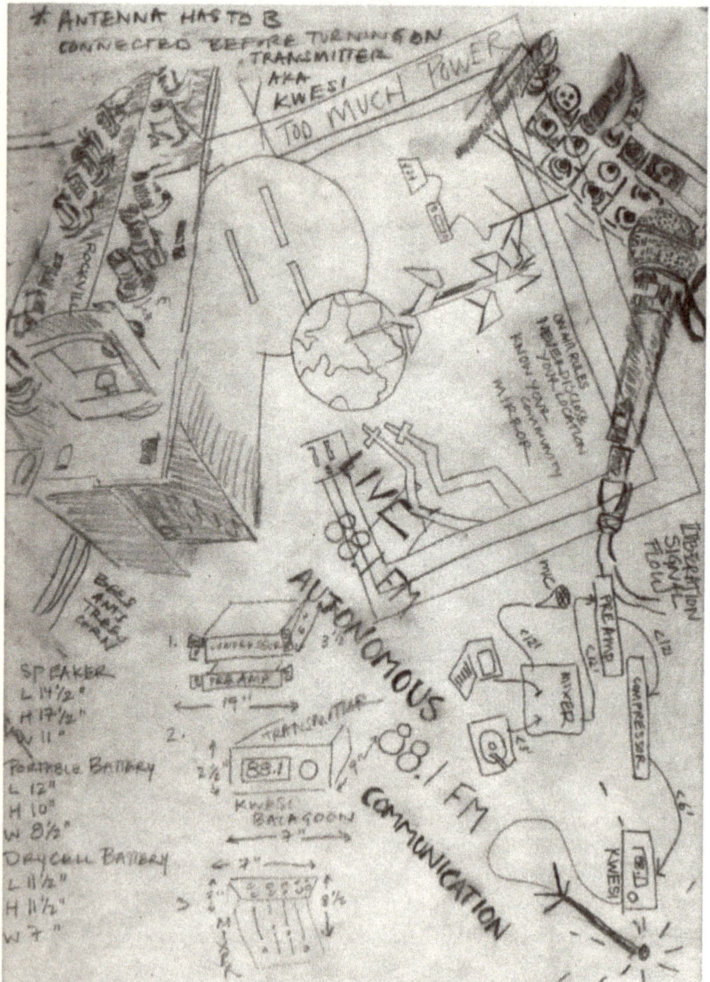
* ANTENNA HAS TO B
CONNECTED BEFORE TURNING ON
TRANSMITTER
AKA
KWESI
TOO MUCH POWER
LIVE
FM
AUTONOMOUS
88.1 FM
COMMUNICATION
LIBERATION SIGNAL FLOW
MIC
PRE AMP
MIXER
COMPRESSOR
KWESI
SPEAKER
L 14½"
H 17½"
W 11"
PORTABLE BATTERY
L 12"
H 10"
W 8½"
DRYCELL BATTERY
L 11½"
H 11½"
W 7"
1.
PRE AMP
19"
2.
TRANSMITTER
88.1
KWESI
BALAGOON
7"
3

Episode 5: Underconstruction ...

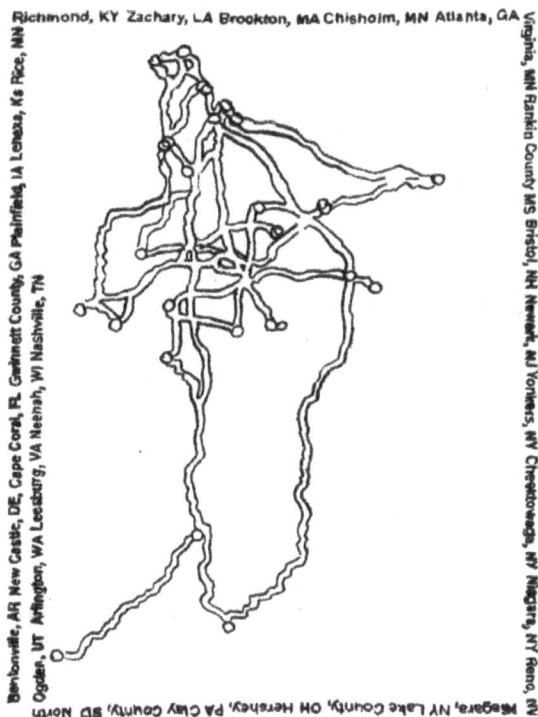

After completing their plotting and planning, dreaming and scheming, hustling and studying, RADIO OUTLAW was ready to roll. Using the power of the people, the bus took off at the least expected time, heading south toward their first target.

Episode 6: For further study ...

- Dread Broadcasting Corporation was the first Black-owned and -controlled station in Europe. To avoid detection, illegal broadcasters transmitted from secret, makeshift studios.[5]

- Mbanna Kantako is the originator of the micro-radio movement. Kantako, a blind Black man from Springfield,

Illinois, started his "pirate" radio station, Human Rights Radio, on November 25, 1987. Starting with just a 1-watt transmitter he bought through a mail-order service, he was able to transmit to roughly eight blocks, enough to reach not only thousands of listeners in the community but the City Hall complex in downtown Springfield as well.[6]

- Robert F. Williams Collection. Radio Free Dixie.[7]

- "We propose in this chapter to study the new attitudes adopted by the Algerian people in the course of the fight for liberation, with respect to a precise technical instrument: the radio. We shall see that what is being called into question behind these new developments in Algerian life is the entire colonial situation. We shall have occasion to show throughout this book that the challenging of the very principle of foreign domination brings about essential mutations in the consciousness of the colonized, in the manner in which he perceives the colonizer, in his human status in the world."[8]

- Good morning, this is Honey. Coming directly to you from Phoenix radio.[9]

- "This book was born from a radio production course. After the practices, they told me anecdotes. They told me how the first program was and how they broke the siege of annihilation. How they evaded the famous goniometers and how the correspondents recorded from the very lines of fire. I met the founders of the radio station, I found out about their love affairs, they revealed to me the secret of Monterrosa's death. They were incredible stories. At first, I listened to them with my mouth open. Then, I opened the recorder and began to order the testimonies from year to year, according to the major stages of the war. Thus, adding stories, this book was born. It is theirs, not mine."[10]

in every home. The only music in most homes was a hand wound Victrola and 78 RPM records. We were allowed in the front room to play the records only on Sunday afternoons. Most of homes had player pianos. We had a piano, none of us could play. I tried, hoping I had talent and would somehow play by ear like some I knew.

I saved from my paper route and bought a Radiola III in 1924. It sat on a table with a separate speaker and Brandeis earphones. ... stations came on the speaker, WT...artford and WBZ, Springfield.

The radio took time to set up. It had a lot of colored wires to connect to A batteries, C batteries, B and D batteries under the table. I figured it out.

I'd stay up late even on school nights, DX...

END BOOK ONE

Conclusion: Democracy's Terrors and our Endless Resistance

Joy James

War and Art, and/or Art of War

For the United States, our most bloody wars in terms of U.S. casualties did not come from World War I or World War II or Vietnam (or other genocidal invasions). Our most devastating war in terms of chaos and loss of life resides in the 1861–1865 Civil War in which some 600,000 died on U.S. soil. In *Black Reconstruction in America* (1935), W.E.B. Du Bois writes that nearly 200,000 people of African descent/Blacks fought in the Civil War, thus the North, with its own distinct racism, prevailed. We also note that the 13th Amendment that "abolished" slavery was in fact a Trojan Horse. Postwar and post-Reconstruction, Black people accused, charged or convicted of a crime could be worked to death as slaves in post-emancipation prison labor. Hence, post-civil war and post-Reconstruction era, we died faster in "freedom" as 20th-century slaves owned by the state and corporate death camps; thus, we rebuilt the infrastructure of the south, and nation through murderous carceral captivity.[1]

In the first quarter of the 21st century, white nationalists and imperialists appear confident that their "confederacy" would/will rise again, through labor exploitation, femicide, genocide, racism and anti-Blackness, terror and repression of GBTQI+ people. Billionaire ballers and authoritarians shred protections and laws that offered some modicum of safety and stability for the mass. Yet, art and resistance continue, as evident in the book cover, chapters and visuals. Our inspirations to struggle have always embraced art and rebellion, care and marronage, communal-protections and self-defense.

During the impending demise of the Third Reich, the French film, *Les Enfants du Paradis* (*The Children of Paradise*), directed by Marcel Carné, emerged in 1943–45. In two parts, the stunning film, set in 1830s Paris, offers a love story and a story of lost love. *The Children of Paradise*, was filmed in collaborationist Vichy France and Occupied France, controlled by the Third Reich. The film was not mere entertainment; it offered an underpinning of rebellion against Nazis and fascists. The storyline elegantly moves beyond personal protagonists and individual villains. The heartbreaking and breathtaking narrative is prepared for and laden with betrayal and resistance. After the last scene of the film was shot and was framed, members of the cast packed up their equipment, gathered their belongings, and proceeded toward the underground to fight fascists, Nazis, enslavers. Amidst repression, mass murders, death camps, and authoritarians, artists created black-and-white romantic drama during a war of 50-80million casualties.

After World War II, European powers would fade in the shadows of a postwar U.S. "superpower." During the Cold War, First World Caligulan cruelties created more killing fields. U.S. democracy battled socialism, communism, trade unionism, Black and Indigenous sovereignty. Through assassinations, School of the Americas death squads, and coups, the U.S. eviscerated Third World liberation movements in Africa, the Middle East, Latin America, the Caribbean, and Asia. It is estimated that U.S. covert and overt global violence took the lives of some 20million "colonized" people of the Third World. (The Soviet Union lost over 20 million people fighting the Third Reich; emerging as the Second World, it supported/financed "Third World" liberation movements.)

As resistors to predatory wars, our "children of paradise" offer intergenerational wisdom. Their artistic and radical sensibilities enable chores, obligations, and passions move from the epicenter towards the hypocenter. Bridging the surface of politics to acknowledge the strategies of the underground— they understand that there are no guarantees that they will be spared from expulsions, imprisonment, disappearance, as actors confront democracy's terrors. Our images, stories, narratives and organizing form collective struggles shaped by art and agape that allow us to survive and thrive.

The streets and screens allow us to glimpse our futures in democracy's devastations. We strategize to build international educational connections to expand our work. For example, the April 2025 People's Tribunal in London, allowed organizers to discuss with communities how "PTSD" (Post-Traumatic Stress Disorder) from UK militarized-police violence is actually "CTSD" (Continuing Trauma Stress Disorder).) Confronting repression, we turn trauma into an informant: take it to tea, dissect its narratives, strategize to curtail emotional flare ups; redirect its terrors and exhaustions that push us to fear (Black) revolutionaries more than we fear predatory states.

Parasitism: CIA/FBI vs. Black Power

The 1960s–70s chant or refrain: "ALL Power to the People!" has remained with us for over half a century. However, the multi-racial or rainbow coalitions that once challenged the state/corporation are disciplined to be steered into the corporate and militarized state. Co-optations of radical analyses and practices are normative. Chicago Black Panther Party leaders Fred Hampton and Mark Clark were assassinated on December 4, 1969 by the FBI and the Chicago Police Department (CPD); one week later, the LAPD, Los Angeles Police Department, tried but failed to kill Panthers in Southern California with the first deployment of SWAT. The Panthers' revolutionary calls for "All Power to the People!" was comprehensive: armed self-defense, mutual aid, housing, food and education, as well as autonomy and the dismantling of colonialism and imperialism. Decades later, Black Chicagoan male elites redirected the legacy of the BPP, from war towards nonprofit earnings and electoral politics in a duopoly democracy. Former aide to Rev. Martin Luther King, Jr., Jesse Jackson founded the "National Rainbow Coalition" in 1984, campaigned as a U.S. DNC presidential candidate in 1988, and served as a shadow delegate from 1991 to 1997 for the District of Columbia, while building his nonprofit PUSH. In 2007, Barack Obama captured the same BPP rainbow concept and turned it into promotional visuals for his 2008 presidential campaign and became the first Black imperial U.S. president.

Chicago Panthers Hampton and Clark had their agency for the people brutally severed by FBI/Chicago police assassinations. Politicians, popular film and academia offer representations of Black radicalism. At times their distortions are repelled by the people. The 2021 film *Judas and the Black Messiah*[2] was originally designed as Hollywood commercial entertainment about the Chicago Panthers. Black Panther intellectualism, compassion and militancy were an afterthought[3] for the filmmakers until Fred Hampton Jr. worked with Macro Productions, and co-producer Ryan Coogler and Warner Brothers, for the film to more accurately depict the agency of his father Fred Hampton and the devastations of COINTEL-PRO. Films, books, nonprofits and academia—as well as state policing— have the capacity to distort the agency and legacy of liberation struggles.

However, the paragon of infiltration and co-optation is the Central Intelligence Agency (CIA). Formed in the 1947 National Security Act, the CIA embodies counterinsurgency. The CIA functioned to derail or destroy communal, socialist/communist, anti-corporate, anti-imperialist and anti-racist organizations. The CIA (along with the FBI) decimated leaders within governments, labor organizations, Indigenous communities through "regime changes"; also known as: coups, assassinations, death squads, and mass disappearances. That is the "hard" counterinsurgency that terrorized the Panthers, American Indian Movement (AIM) and radicals also collaborated with the "soft" counterinsurgency that siphoned the political identities and agency of militants. A transfusion of non-militants settled into nonprofits and academia. The CIA and FBI developed terrorist tactics to destroy (proto-) revolutionary societies. They cushioned democracy's terrors with "soft" counterinsurgency in which funding publications, intellectuals, films, nonprofits and academics would (re)shape radical culture into liberal displays while directing "Black militancy" into a two-party duopoly of capitalism and imperialism. The "soft" counterinsurgency often consists of capturing Black rebellion and freedom.

On September 7, 2022, the CIA unveiled its statue of Harriet Tubman in their quad (the bronze statue is a replica of Brian Hanlon's sculpture at the New York State Equal Rights Heritage

Center). The Agency celebrated her on their 75th anniversary, stating that Tubman was one of "their" spies during the civil war, a key figure who fought for the North. Born Araminta Ross (1822– 1913), named "General Tubman" and "Moses," her revolutionary resistance to enslavement was foundational; the CIA does not note that she offered assistance to John Brown's 1859 revolutionary insurrection at Harper Ferry. The CIA dedication ceremony at its headquarters included Tubman's distant relatives, Hanlon, and the Superintendent of the Harriet Tubman Underground Railroad. How we would liberate our ancestors, and ourselves, and shape our desires for freedom through intellectual, political, and spiritual struggles and journeys?

Attempting to free radical movements from capture, we remain mindful that as nonprofits and digital platforms become more dependent on external funders, claims to "community-based" allegiance have accountability issues. Nonprofits can hire members of the working class without allowing them to unionize the nonprofits, and thus rendering them dependent upon jobs paid for by state/ (non)corporate donors. (*Beyond Cop Cities* notes some contradictions when nonprofits receive millions of dollars under the guise of leading liberation endeavors, see *BCC*, p.113, note 2.)

The meaning of the "Black Radical Tradition" (BRT) is contested. Some prominent academics and abolitionists assert that President Barack Obama is part of BRT leadership while Panther vets such as Glen Ford and Dhoruba Bin-Wahad critique powerful elites, and all POTUSES, including Obama, as counterinsurgent or imperial actors. Panther intellectuals, Ford and Bin-Wahad describe academia and nonprofits connected to wealthy, politically-connected donors as destabilizing (Black) revolutionary struggles.

A half century after Hampton and Clark were killed by the U.S. state,[4] Black Panther veteran Glen Ford (1949–2021)[5] transitioned from the material world the year Hollywood displayed its commercialized film on Chicago Panthers. In 2021, Glen Ford's *The Black Agenda* offered cutting analyses of Black freedom struggles:

If anything has been learned from the past half century of Black reliance on Democratic Party politicians, it is that no lasting victories can be achieved without the transfer of control of public resources directly to the people. That was the meaning of "All Power to the People" when the phrase was coined, and must remain the goal of the movement today. (p. 324)

Ford popularized the phrase "Black Mis-leadership," analyzing how political struggles become coopted by corporate donors and politicians. His final chapter in *The Black Agenda*, "Part X, Black Lives Matter, Reparations, and a New Authentic Left," offers essays, from 2015–2019, which are largely critical as evident in their titles: "#BlackLivesMatter and the Democrats: How Disruption Can Lead to Collaboration"; "#BlackLivesMatter Performs a Self-Humiliation at Hillary Clinton's Hands"; "Black Lives Matter Groups Hoping for a Big Payday"; "Black Lives Matter Founder Launches Huge Project to Shrink Black Lives."

Ford's June 10, 2015, essay "Democrats Hope to Bury Black Lives Matter under Election Blitz," is unambiguous:

[T]he Democratic Party sits atop the Black polity "like a grotesque Sumo wrestler," squeezing out the Black radical tradition. The Black Lives Matter movement consciously draws on this authentic – and still deeply honored – radical tradition, seeking to put it into practice under 21st century conditions.

Some seven years later, after BLM (and funding) expanded following the 2020 George Floyd tragedy, the meaning of "Democrats Hope to Bury Black Lives Matter..." was "captured." An excised sentence distorted and decontextualized Ford's analyses. What Ford critiqued as flaws becomes reworked by other writers into a celebratory embrace of the conventional BLM. Thus, the "Black Radical Tradition" loses its moorings and the meaning of "Black resistance" dissipates into the liberatory "mainstream" of progressive academia:

Likewise, as BLM was consolidating, the radical journalist and organizer Glen Ford contended, "the Black Lives Matter movement consciously draws on this authentic—and still deeply

147

honored—radical tradition, seeking to put it into practice under 21st century conditions" not least by resisting the criminal legal system, prioritizing social and economic transformation, and demanding global peace. (Charisse Burden-Stelly, *Black Scare / Red Scare* [p. 246] excerpt from Ford, "Democrats Hope to Bury Black Lives Matter under Election Blitz")

Glen Ford did not celebrate BLM for "resisting the criminal legal system, prioritizing social and economic transformation, and demanding global peace" (Burden-Stelly). Although BLM provides advocacy and support within activist and nonprofit structures, Ford forecasted that Black nonprofits—funded by state/corporation and amplified by academia and pundits— would consolidate formations to claim "radicalism" but in practice would align with anti-revolutionary funders/donors/influencers. For Ford, it was inevitable that (Black) radical agency would decline under such conditions of capture and distortion, and so he closes his article with a poignant prediction:

> [The] 2015 Black Lives Matter movement has no institutional stake in the victory of either party, but is, in fact, locked in mortal political struggle with other Black people in the Democratic Party. These Black Democrats will insist on a truce, a cessation of agitation against national or local Democrats, until after the election. As with the Occupy movement, this will be accompanied by intensified police pressures against activists. At the end of the process, the Black Lives Matter movement is meant to go the way of Occupy, lost in the electoral Mardis Gras – killed by Democrats, not Republicans.

Dhoruba Bin-Wahad's analysis of "Black counterinsurgency" and encapsulation is aligned with Glen Ford's concept of "Black Mis-leadership." Both Panther veterans warned that nonprofit corporations and academia—steered by donors and statecraft— would denature (Black) revolutionary struggles. Affluent academics, nonprofits, pundits, authors, media, major press and publishers can with ease extract from and popularize revolutionary language but not pursue a revolutionary strategy that would lead to less popularity and less payouts. After nineteen years as a political prisoner, incarcerated on fabricated charges, Bin-Wahad critiques our movements and "encapsulation." *Revolution in These Times: Black Panther Party Veteran Dhoruba Bin-Wahad on Antifascism, Black Liberation, and a Culture of Resistance* (2025) interrogates our capacity to confront fascism. For Bin-Wahad, nonprofits, liberal politicians, and academia are key in "encapsulating the idea and the notion of the Black Liberation Movement," subduing its "rage ... momentum" (p.53). Nonprofits and mass media have capacity to "[re]brand" militancy to support the interests of academia/corporation/state:

Why would we name the movement after a structurally impossible aspiration ["Black Lives Matter"]? ... We must understand the tactic of counterrevolutionary politics and the use of encapsulation of organizations by the state. Encapsulation is a process by which the enemy—those in power—create movements that they can control and direct and siphon off the energy ... [that can function] in a revolutionary fashion ... (Bin-Wahad, p. 116)

Revolution in These Times dissects state/corporate strategies deployed against organizing that rejects state/corporate/nonprofit capture. In Chapter 6, "The Limitations of a Hashtag Movement," Bin-Wahad critiques the contradictions within which we name and identify ourselves as "radical activists." Bin-Wahad argues that liberal-left advocates were able to "encapsulate a movement by centering organizations and individuals that seem to personify what the movement stands for"; yet, money and influence steered activists towards the state and corporations to develop "advocates of electoral politics" or prominent spokespeople for civil/human rights. Bin-Wahad asserts that any "hashtag movement" can become "a means of encapsulating the rage and the righteous struggle"; any "movement" is vulnerable to being "hijacked"; and so, "an entire generation's understanding of their militant and radical history" becomes distorted (p. 116). He notes the international global freedom struggles hampered by influential funders: "If you said it was a Black Liberation Movement and you were in solidarity with other peoples' movement[s] in Palestine, in Africa and in Asia, you weren't getting no money from [billionaire investor and philanthropist George] Soros and [billionaire Jeff Bezos's] Amazon" (pps.117-118). Bin-Wahad also notes that our movements lack radical resources and protections:

> Encapsulation of our movement goes hand in hand with physical repression and intimidation, and that's where the armed agents of the state come in. . . . We have lawyers who are not political enough to understand a strategic vision of how to practice law in a way that empowers our people, in a way that brings out the con-tradictions of the system so that our people could be organized around those contradictions (pps.121-122).

Coda

In spite of limitations and deficiencies, agape continues to shape our moves and movements to confront racism, sexism, anti-LGBTQI+ stalkers, violence against the environment, children, women, men, nonbinary peoples. With communities stranded in poverty, traf-ficking, deportations, detention camps, environmental destruction, wars and genocide, we continue to create, confront, resist, and defeat predatory violence.[6]

Through communal caretaking, protest, movement making, mar-ronage, war resistance, and sanctuary, Captive Maternals love and labor. With spirituality and ancestral teachings, we learn to lean into the past, present, and future. We recognize the countless sacrifices of others such as Ana Mae Aquash[7], Assata Shakur[8], Aaron Busnell[9].

Confronting counterinsurgency—waving the colors of rainbow warriors—we travel from the surface of struggles into the under-grounds in order to protect and heal life, land, and culture.

Contributors

Mohamed Abdou is an intellectual and an author and professor. He has taught at Cornell University and Columbia University and educated students in encampments seeking to stop genocidal wars and create safety for educational and ethical learning. Abdou is author of *Islam and Anarchism* (Pluto, 2022).

susan abulhawa is an author, poet, scientist, mother, and activist. Her writings include the novels *Mornings in Jenin*, *The Blue Between Sky and Water*, and *Against the Loveless World*, and the poetry collection, *My Voice Sought the Wind*. abulhawa advocates for animal rights and liberation, and ecological conservation. She is also the founder of Playgrounds for Palestine and is the Executive Director of the Palestine Writes Literary Festival.

Ashanti Omowali Alston an anarchist activist, speaker, and writer, and a veteran of the Black Panther Party and Black Liberation Army, serves on the Steering Committee of the Jericho Movement to free U.S. political prisoners.

kai barrow is a visual artist based in New Orleans. barrow has worked with FIERCE (a New York City-based LGBTQ youth organization), Critical Resistance, Southerners on New Ground. barrow is co-founder of the Radio Outlaw project in New Orleans and works with NYC ACT ONE: THE BOOK OF AIR of Gallery of the Streets' multi-part project, *[b]REACH: adventures in heterotopia, a Black surrealist opera*, and with Radio Outlaw, a mobile autonomous communication system.

Chris Browne leads the "Radicals in Conversation" podcast for Pluto Press. He is also an artist, musician and author.

Maurice Carney is co-founder and Executive Director of the Friends of the Congo and fought with the Congolese people for several decades. He is a journalist and writer for Real News Network.

Liliana is an immigrant from Colombia based in Houston, Texas. An abolitionist, she has worked directly with prisoners on death row. She is the co-host of the radio show 'Voz de La Tierra' on KPFT Pacifica, discussing the geopolitical effects of militarism, policing, imperialism, and racism on Indigenous, Black, and immigrant colonized communities.

Kalonji Changa, an organizer and founder of the FTP Movement and Black Power Media, is author of *How to Build a People's Army* and editor of *Revolution in These Times: Black Panther Party Veteran Dhoruba bin Wahad on Antifascism, Black Liberation, and a Culture of Resistance.* A contributor to *Beyond Cop Cities*, and co-producer of the documentary *Organizing Is the New Cool*, he serves as co-chair of the Urban Survival and Preparedness Institute.

Andréia Beatriz dos Santos, co-author of *Rise Up or Die!*, is a co-founder and main organizer of Reja ou Será Morto/Reaja ou Será Morta (Rise Up or Die!). She is trained as a medical doctor.

Hamilton Borges dos Santos is a co-founder and main organizer of Reja ou Será Morto/Reaja ou Será Morta (Rise Up or Die!). Hamilton is a poet, writer, amateur gardener. He is co-author of *Rise Up or Die!*

Jazz Franklin is a filmmaker and artist and co-founder of the Radio Outlaw project based in New Orleans and works with NYC ACT ONE: THE BOOK OF AIR of Gallery of the Streets'. Franklin has worked on the *House of Tulip*, a documentary about the dangers of being Trans in the America (profiled in *Time Magazine*—https://time.com/6320075/house-of-tulip-documentary/).

Claude Gatebuke, a survivor of the Rwandan genocide, is Executive Director of the African Great Lakes Action Network.

rosalind hampton is an associate professor of Black Studies in the Department of Social Justice Education at the Ontario Institute for Studies in Education. Professor hampton's areas of teaching and research include Black radical thought, arts, critical-creative practice; Black Studies in Canadian higher education, student activism, and community-based and popular education. hampton is the author of *Black Racialization and Resistance at an Elite University.*

Joy James is Ebenezer Fitch Professor of the Humanities at Williams College. Her most recent books include: *In Pursuit of Revolutionary Love*; *New Bones Abolition*; and *Contextualizing Angela Davis.* James is the editor of *Beyond Cop Cities*; *ENGAGE: Indigenous, Black and Afro-Indigenous Futures.* She works with the People's Tribunal https://peoples-tribunal.org/.

Kara Lynch is a time-based artist living in the Bronx, NY—born in the momentous year of 1968. Kara completed the MFA in Visual Arts at the University of California, San Diego and has been a research fellow at the African and African Diaspora Studies Department, University of Texas Austin and the Academy of African Studies at Bayreuth University in Germany. She is an emerita Professor of Video and Critical Studies at Hampshire College. In 2020 Kara was awarded a Tulsa Artist Fellowship and joined Gallery of the Streets as a principled artist collaborator. Lynch is co-founder of the Radio Outlaw project in New Orleans and works with NYC ACT ONE: THE BOOK OF AIR of Gallery of the Streets.

Rev. Keyanna Jones Moore is a Political and Social Justice Activist, Community Organizer and Movement Trainer from Atlanta, Georgia. She currently serves as Co-Pastor of Park Avenue Baptist Church (Atlanta, GA), where she organizes at the intersection of faith and justice. She is the proprietor of E Equals MC Squared Educational Services, LLC, where she works as a Homeschool Curriculum Consultant, IEP Advocate and German Translator. Keyanna is the wife of Jerrod Moore and mother to their unique and extraordinary children.

Dr. Ikemba Ojore is an assistant Professor at Medgar Evers College in NY, Ikemba Ojore and co-founder of the AKERELE Leadership Academy. He chairs the We Charge Colonialism Media and Think Tank, and is co-host of the Rise Up Show on Black Power Media. Ojore serves on the Malcolm X Day Committee and works with the NYC branch of the International People's Democratic Uhuru Movement.

Brother Passy is a member of Friends of the Congo and works with Pan African solidarity organizations to increase global consciousness about the Congo's challenges and potential of the Congo

Benjamin Ramos Rosado is a Boricua lover of food and liberation. An advocate for Puerto Rican liberation, Ramos Rosado educates, organizes, and mobilizes for various revolutionary causes.

joão costa vargas is a professor of Anthropology and Black Studies at the University of California—Riverside. He is the author of: *Catching Hell in the City of Angels*; *Never Meant to Survive*; *The Denial of Antiblackness: Multiracial Redemption and Black Suffering*. He is co-editor of *State of White Supremacy* and *Anti-Blackness*. His written work draws from collaborative projects in Rio de Janeiro, São Paulo, and Salvador (in Brazil), as well as Austin and Los Angeles (in the U.S.).

Kwame Wilburg is a member of Friends of the Congo.

Notes

Preface

1. See Norman Ohler, *Blitzed: Drugs in Nazi Germany* and *Tripped: Nazi Germany, the CIA, and the Dawn of the Psychedelic Age.*
2. For educational tutorials on counterinsurgency and police/military violence, see: "Twisted Laws: Mumia, Universities and Palestine," April 24, 2025, www.youtube.com/watch?v=LD7OL8X9PMM; and, The People's Tribunal on Police Killings, London, UK, April 4–5, 2025, https://peoples-tribunal.org/
3. Gaius Caesar Germanicus, emperor of the Roman Empire, 37–41 CE.

Introduction

1. Edited by Joy James, published by Pluto Press.
2. As an alternative to White Christian Nationalism, Creation Covenant Alliance offers a critique of Project 2025 (co-)led by the Heritage Foundation. See Dana Drugmand, "Project 2025: Inside Trump's Plan to Bulldoze American Climate Policy," Creation Covenant Alliance. For a summary of White Christian Nationalism, see "Understanding White Christian Nationalism," Yale ISPS, October 4, 2022.
3. On December 17, 2024, media reported that the parents of environmental and social justice activist Manuel Paez Teran— "Tortuguita"—filed "a lawsuit ... against three law enforcement officers; the parents asserted that the police raid led to [Tortuguita's] January 2023 death and violation of the fourth amendment" (Timothy Pratt, "Family of 'Cop City' Activist Shot Dead by Georgia Police Sue Officers Involved," *The Guardian*, December 17, 2024).
   Charges made by defense attorneys include police and troopers' violations of First Amendment rights of activists and organizers. Atlanta police have jurisdiction only over the Cop City site, not the park forest; defense attorneys for Stop Cop City protesters, environmentalists and abolitionists assert that three Georgia Bureau of Investigation officers and state patrol officers engaged in "false arrests," and violation of the fourth amendment (see Pratt, "Family of 'Cop City' Activist Shot Dead by Georgia Police Sue Officers Involved"; see also Pratt,

"Georgia Refuses to Release Evidence from Police Shooting of Cop City Activist," *The Guardian*, October 16, 2023).

4. See: www.blackpast.org/global-african-history/primary-documents-global-african-history/we-charge-genocide-historic-petition-united-nations-relief-crime-united-states-government-against/

5. This is analyzed in "52nd Anniversary of Wounded Knee: Remembering Perry Ray Robinson," Black Power Media, www.youtube.com/watch?v=3dSnb3YUNxU

6. Mahmoud Khalil, "I Am a Palestinian Political Prisoner in the US. I Am Being Targeted for My Activism," *The Guardian*, March 19, 2025

7. See: www.workers.org/2024/12/82417/

8. Dana Drugmand, "Project 2025, Inside Trump's Plan to Bulldoze American Climate Policy," Creation Covenant Alliance, May 30, 2024.

9. See: www.thejerichomovement.com/

10. Mahmoud Khalil, the most prominent of the detainees, was a student at Columbia University and is currently held in a Louisiana ICE facility based on free speech criticizing genocide of Palestinian. He was prevented from being with his wife Dr. Noor Abdalla to attend the birth of their first child in April 2025. See "A Letter from Palestinian Activist Mahmoud Khalil," ACLU, March 20, 2025.

11. Anna Betts, "Mohsen Mahdawi, Palestinian Green-card Holder and Columbia Student, Detained by ICE," *The Guardian*, April 14, 2025.

12. Sharon Zang, "Tufts Student Activist Rumeysa Ozturk Abducted by ICE on Her Way to Iftar," *TRUTHOUT*, March 26, 2025.

13. "Close to 2,000 Environmental Activists Killed Over Last Decade," *Yale Environment 360*, September 13, 2023.

14. "In Memory of Ken Saro-Wiwa," PEN, England, www.englishpen.org/posts/campaigns/in-memory-of-ken-saro-wiwa/

15. Khury Petersen-Smith and Hannah Homestead, "Fact Sheet. Genocide in Gaza—The Biden Administration's Role and Legacy," Institute for Policy Studies, December 17, 2024, https://ips-dc.org/fact-sheet-genocide-in-gaza-the-biden-administrations-role-and-legacy/

16. Published by Pluto Press, 2022.

1   Atlanta's Black Community Says "Stop Cop Cities!"

1. Margaret Kimberley, interview with Rev. Keyanna Jones, *Black Agenda Report*, 2023. www.blackagendareport.com/atlantas-black-community-says-stop-cop-city

    Rev. Keyanna Jones concludes the *BAR* interview by referencing a 2023 conference and week of action against Cop City, sponsored by communitymovementbuilders.org, yet later departed from the organization which reportedly received several million dollars.

2 Resisting [Global] Cop Cities and the Militarization of Policing

1. This chapter is an edited transcript of a September 30, 2024, Pluto Podcast of "Radicals in Conversation," hosted by Chris Browne, discussing *Beyond Cop Cities: Dismantling State and Corporate-Funded Armies and Prisons*. Podcast notes correct errors in *Beyond Cop Cities*: the surname of political prisoner is Joy *Powell* (misprinted as "Power"); Tortuguita reportedly had over 50 gunshot wounds in their body, but likely was shot by Georgia state troopers a dozen times; media attributed all October 7, 2023, deaths to Hamas; however, investigative journalists report that Israeli military "friendly fire" likely killed an unknown number of hostages, noncombatants and foreign workers.
2. Edited by Joy James, published by Pluto Press.
3. "Dec. 11, 1981: El Mozote Massacre in El Salvador," Zinn Education Project: Teaching People's History, www.zinnedproject.org/news/tdih/el-mozote-massacre-in-el-salvador/.
4. "The Overthrow of Democracy in Chile—A Timeline," Zinn Education Project, www.zinnedproject.org/materials/chile-coup-timeline/
5. "Mass Graves of Immigrants Found in Texas, but State Says No Laws Were Broken," *Democracy Now!* July 16, 2015, www.democracynow.org/2015/7/16/mass_graves_of_immigrants_found_in#:~:text=Texas%20says%20othere%20is%20%E2%80%9Cno,%2C%20Texas%2C%20in%20Brooks%20County.

3 1492: Indigenous Sovereignty, Black Self-Determination and Repression

1. This chapter comes from a transcript from Black Power Media/Guerrilla Intellectual University 2024 interview of Momodou Abion and Ashanti Alston with Kalonji Changa and Joy James.
2. Bill Bigelow, "Teaching the Seeds of Violence in Palestine-Israel," Zinn Education Project, 2024, www.zinnedproject.org/materials/teaching-the-seeds-of-violence-in-palestine-israel/
3. See authors: Frantz Fanon, *Black Skin, White Masks*; Hamid Dabashi, *Brown Skin, White Masks*; and Glen Coulthard, *Red Skin, White Masks*.
4. Kwame Ture in this clip states that religion and revolution "go hand-in-hand": www.instagram.com/aaprpinternational/reel/CzqqA9WucRp/. There are revolutionaries who may not be religious in a formal sense.

5. See Joy James, *New Bones Abolition: Captive Maternal Agency and the Afterlife of Erica Garner*, Common Notions, 2023.
6. Adam Zeidan, "Abraham Accords," *Encyclopedia Britannica*, www.britannica.com/topic/Abraham-Accords, updated April 2025.

4 Presentation to the UN Special Committee on Decolonization: Puerto Rico

1. "July 25, 1898: U.S. Invades Puerto Rico," Zinn Education Project, www.zinnedproject.org/news/tdih/us-invades-puerto-rico/
2. See *La Operación* (documentary film, 1982), Zinn Education Project, www.zinnedproject.org/collection/puerto-rico/

5 Oxford Union Address on Genocide, Israel, Palestine

1. Rasha Khatib, Martin McKee, and Salim Yusuf, "Counting the Dead in Gaza: Difficult but Essential," *The Lancet*, 404(10449): 237–238, July 20, 2024, reports that by June 19, 2024, Israel's invasion into Gaza had led to the deaths of 37,396 people. Public Health Situation Analysis (PHSA) on "Hostilities in the Palestinian territory," (oPt) May 2, 2024, states that from October 7, 2023 to April 30, 2024, the Israeli military killed 34,568 and injured 77,765 Palestinians. The *PBS* (Public Broadcasting System) in the U.S. reports in late April 2025 that Israel's military offensive has killed more than 52,000 Palestinians, the majority women and children, since October 2023. See: "Israeli Strikes on Gaza Kills as War Drags on with No End in Sight," *PBS News World*, April 28, 2025.

6 Fighting for the Congo

1. See: Jude Bela, "The REAL Reason Rwanda Is Invading DR Congo," *InvideoAI*, February 2025, www.youtube.com/watch?v=IMoYZoiNwm4
2. See "Africa's World War: The Congo War", History Guild, May 13, 2021, https://historyguild.org/africas-world-war-the-congo-war/
3. See, "5 Things to Know about the Fighting in the Democratic of Congo", *NPR*, January 31, 2025, www.npr.org/2025/01/31/nx-s1-5281422/congo-goma-fighting-m23-rwanda-drc
4. "Kagame's Hidden War in the Congo", *The New York Review of Books*, September 2009, https://archive.globalpolicy.org/security-council/index-of-countries-on-the-security-council-agenda/democratic-republic-of-congo/48118-kagames-hidden-war-in-the-congo.html

5. Marie Toulemonde, "Rubaya, Coltan Mine: Blood Minerals: DRCRwanda: Rubaya Coltan Mine at the Heart of M23 Financing," *The Africa Report*, February 6, 2025, www.theafricareport.com/375904/drc-rwanda-rubaya-coltan-mine-at-the-heart-of-m23-financing/

6. "(Southern African Development Community): www.google.com/search?q=sadc&oq="&gs_lcrp=EgZjaHJvbWUqEggAEAAYQxiDARixAxiABBiKBTISCAAQABhDGIMBGLEDGIAEGIoFMgcIARAAGIAEMgcIAhAAGIAEMgcIAxAAGIAEMgcIBBAAGIAEMgcIBRAAGIAEMgcIBhAAGIAEMgcIBxAAGIAEMgcICBAAGIAEMgcICRAAGIAEogEIMTkzNGowajSoAgCwAgE&sourceid=chrome&ie=UTF-8

7. MONUSCO is the United Nations Organization Stabilization Mission in the DRC.

8. Sophie Neiman, "'We Are All on the Front Line': DR Congo's Young Women Rebels Take on M23," *Al Jazeera*, August 14, 2024; Wazalendo coalition.

9. For Paul Kagame, see Peter Beaumont, "Rwanda: Human Rights Fears in Nation whose Leader Faces Murder Claims," *The Guardian*, April 14, 2022. For Yoweri Museveni, see *BBC*, www.bbc.com/news/topics/c6mkk7dqljet; Amnesty International, "Uganda: President's Approval of Anti-LGBTQI Bill is a Grave Assault on Human Rights," May 29, 2023, www.amnesty.org/en/latest/news/2023/05/presidents-musevenis-approval-of-anti-lgbti-bill-is-a-assault-on-human-rights/; Amnesty International, *Uganda 2023*, www.amnesty.org/en/location/africa/east-africa-the-horn-and-great-lakes/uganda/report-uganda/; Amnesty International, *Democratic Republic of Congo*, www.amnesty.org/en/location/africa/east-africa-the-horn-and-great-lakes/uganda/report-uganda/; Amnesty International, *CONGO 2023*. www.amnesty.org/en/location/africa/west-and-central-africa/congo/report-congo/

10. Sanctions against Russia, not the same against Rwanda: U.S. Department of the Treasury, "Treasury Intensifies Sanctions Targeting Russia's Oil Production and Exports," January 10, 2025, https://home.treasury.gov/news/press-releases/jy2777

11. Shola Lawal, "A Guide to the Decades-long Conflict in DR Congo," *Al Jazeera*, February 21, 2024. www.aljazeera.com/news/2024/2/21/a-guide-to-the-decades-long-conflict-in-dr-congo; "M23 conflict caused nearly 3 out of every 4 displacements in the DRC this year," IDMC (Internal Displacement Monitoring Centre, September 23, 2024, www.internal-displacement.org/expert-analysis/m23-conflict-caused-nearly-3-out-of-every-4-displacements-in-the-drc-this-year/

12. Kwame Nkrumah, *The Challenge of Congo*, 1969, https://openlibrary.org/works/OL2139443W/Challenge_of_the_Congo?edition=key%3A%2Fbooks%2FOL28116371M

13. Ernesto "Che" Guevara, *The Diaries of Ernesto Che Guevara*, www.marxists.org/archive/guevara/works.htmrecord

14. Congo was created by colonizers: see 1884–85 Berlin Conference and the terror reign of Leopold II, King of the Belgians. See also Alison Kysia, "Congo, Coltan, and Cell Phones: A People's History," Zinn Education Project.

7   The Prisoner Human Rights Movement: 2025 Nobel Letter

1. See: https://ccrjustice.org/sites/default/files/attach/2015/07/Agreement%20to%20End%20Hostilities.pdf

8   The Abolition of Carceral Schooling

1. "Panther Pedagogy: Kim Holder," in Joy James (ed.) *Engage: Indigenous, Black and Afro-Indigenous Futures*, London: Pluto Press, 2025, p. 232.

9   Black (Brazilian) Futurity

1. This chapter is an excerpt from *Rise Up or Die!* by Hamilton dos Santos, Andréia Beatriz dos Santos and João Costa Vargas, Philadelphia: Common Notions Press, 2025.

2. In Afro-Brazilian rituals, the Alabê is the person responsible for playing the atabaque, a tall wooden hand drum.

3. President Lula's third inauguration took place on January 1, 2023. See "Lula Sworn In as President of Divided Brazil Amid Tight Security," *Al Jazeera*, January 1, 2023, www.aljazeera.com/news/2023/1/1/lula-inauguration-president-brazil

4. On the legal debate on the 1916 Civil Code between Barbosa and Bevilaqua, see Gisele M. Salgado, "Discussões Legislativas do Código Civil de 1916: Uma Revisão Historiográfica," *Revista Eletrônica da Faculdade de Direito da Universidade Federal do Pelotas* 5(1, Jan.–Jul 2019): 40–84.

5. "Brazilian Football Legend Pele Dies at Age 82," *Al Jazeera*, December 29, 2022, www.aljazeera.com/news/2022/12/29/brazilian-football-legend-pele-dies-aged-82

6. Eliana Alves Cruz, "Para o Homem Negro que Viveu Dentro de Pelé," *Folha de S. Paulo*, December 29, 2022, www1.folha.uol.com.br/

esporte/2022/12/para-o-homem-negro-que-vive-dentro-do-pele. shtml

7. The manifestos are available from Rise Up's website: https:// reajanasruas.blogspot.com

8. Naiara Galarraga Cortázar, "The Color of Politics in Brazil," *El País*, September 25, 2022, https://english.elpais.com/international/ 2022-09-25/the-color-of-politics-in-brazil.html

9. Ministério do Desenvolvimento e Assistência Social, Família e Combate à Fome.

10   When Opportunity Knocks ...

1. "Ten Minutes of Static," www.youtube.com/watch?v=mfycQJrzXCA

2. "Steal Away/Athan (Call to Prayer)/Fatiha (Sura Prayer)," www. youtube.com/watch?v=NVrs9VeFasM

3. "There It Is," www.youtube.com/watch?v=G6bKgljhvRo

4. "Triptych: Prayer/Protest/Peace (Remastered)," www.youtube.com/ watch?v=tGCt9U7gQFk

5. The pirate station that changed British radio: www.youtube.com/ watch?v=NGQoOaIoRis

6. See: https://everything2.com/title/Mbanna%2BKantako

7. See: https://search.freedomarchives.org/search.php?view_collection=8 &no_digital=1&title=Radio+Free+Dixie

8. See: "This Is the Voice of Algeria," Frantz Fanon, *A Dying Colonialism*, p. 69.

9. See Lizzie Borden, *Born in Flames* and Frimpsy/M.A.S. Frimm, "Where is Honey?" https://medium.com/%40frimpizm101/where-is-honey-cde44fc8ba7b

10. See, José Ignacio López Vigil, *The Thousand and One Stories of Radio Venceremos*.

Conclusion: Democracy's Terrors and Our Endless Resistance

1. To comprehend the scope of U.S. military, counterinsurgency violence that created and prolonged warfare and genocides see *Discriminate Deterrence: The Commission on Integrated Long-Term Strategy*—a 1988 USA manual produced by state elites such as Henry Kissinger, Zbigniew Brzezinski, et. al. U.S. from academia, CIA and the Cold War era that sought to reinstate colonial capture. See: www. airandspaceforces.com/PDF/DocumentFile/Documents/2008/ DiscriminateDeterrence_010188.pdf

2. Meilan Solly, "The History of Judas and the Black Messiah," *Smithsonian Magazine*, February 11, 2021, www.smithsonianmag.com/history/true-history-behind-judas-and-black-messiah-180976975/; *Judas and the Black Messiah*, 2021, www.youtube.com/watch?v=6ivHf4ODMi4

3. See: Glen Ford, *The Black Agenda*, New York/London: OR Books, 2021, 2022; Glen Ford, "Democrats Hope to Bury Black Lives Matter under Election Blitz," June 10, 2015, https://blackagendareport.com/democrats_to_bury_black_lives_matter_under_election. Also see Charisse Burden-Stelly, *Black Scare / Red Scare*, Chicago: University of Chicago Press, 2023.

   Professor and journalist Jared Ball worked with Glen Ford and Dhoruba Bin-Wahad. Ball's March 30, 2024, *imixwhatilike* podcast —"Glen Ford, *Black Scare, Red Scare*, and #BLM"—critiques academic conflation of Panther vet Ford and BLM. <https://www.instagram.com/imixwhatilike/p/C5JiBnJJq22/> On March 31, 2024, after this editor emailed Ball about his critical podcast, Ball's email response expressed concerns about scholarship, distortions of Glen Ford, and academia "misusing Dhoruba [Bin-Wahad] to somehow twist BLM [Black Lives Matter] into being the logical extension of the BLA [Black Liberation Army]". The "Glen Ford, *Black Scare, Red Scare*, and #BLM" podcast appears to have been removed from online in 2024 and remains unavailable as of May 2025.

4. Margaret Kimberley's preface to Ford's *The Black Agenda*, remains faithful to his revolutionary's politics:

   > Glen Ford is irreplaceable not just because his writing was so sharp and so clear, but also because his politics were so clearly of the left. He was not a liberal, or a Democrat, or a progressive. He was a Marxist, and he brought that ideology to all that he did. In so doing he revealed important information that is regularly disregarded or disappeared. He also had a talent for making every issue understandable and making connections with the reality of people's lives. (p. xii)

   Glen Ford co-founded *The Black Agenda Report* (*BAR*) with Bruce Dixon and Margaret Kimberley. His interviews/commentaries are not always easily found on line. See Margaret Kimberley, "Glen Ford's Irreplaceable Journalism," *Black Agenda Report*, July 27, 2022; www.blackagendareport.com/glen-ford-revolutionary-friend-leader-lover-black-people.

5. B.A. Parker et al., "How Three Unlikely Groups Worked Together to Achieve Interracial Solidarity," *Code Switch*, January 25, 2023, www.npr.

org/sections/codeswitch/2023/01/23/1150867899/how-the-rainbow-coalition-was-formed-and-its-legacy

6. See: William I. Robinson, "Crisis for the Contras," *Guardian*, June 13, 1984, chrome-extension://efaidnbmnnnibpcajpcglclefindmkaj/www.cia.gov/readingroom/docs/CIA-RDP90-00845R000100380007-9.pdf

7. See Anna Mae Aquash, "I Believe in the Laws of Nature," Statement to the Court of South Dakota, September 1975, posted *History Is a Weapon* https://historyisaweapon.com/defcon1/aquashlawsofnature.html

8. Assata Shakur, "Women in Prison, How It Is with Us," *The Black Scholar*, April 1978, posted *History Is a Weapon*, https://www.historyisaweapon.com/defcon1/shakurwip.html

9. Statement on the Self-Immolation of Airman Aaron Bushnell, Lemkin Institute, March 7, 2024. https://www.lemkininstitute.com/statements-new-page/statement-on-the-self-immolation-of-airman-aaron-bushnell-

The Pluto Press Newsletter

Hello friend of Pluto!

Want to stay on top of the best radical books
we publish?

Then sign up to be the first to hear about our
new books, as well as special events,
podcasts and videos.

You'll also get 50% off your first order with us
when you sign up.

Come and join us!

Go to bit.ly/PlutoNewsletter